A Life
Worth Becoming

Joseph

Copyright © 2007, Next Innovations

ISBN 978-0-9797732-0-4

LCCN 2007930992

All rights reserved. No part of this book may be reproduced or transmitted in any form or by any means, electronic or mechanical, including photocopying, recording, or by information storage and retrieval systems, without the written permission of the publisher, except by a reviewer who may quote brief passages in a review.

Printed in the United States of America

To Dad
Now passed,
Who gave all he could.

To Mom
Fully alive,
Whose love has never failed.

Table of Contents

Preface   vii

Introduction   ix

Chapter 1:   I Want You
              (Grace)   1

Chapter 2:   But Not To Myself Alone
              (Friendship)   33

Chapter 3:   That New Might Come
              (Innovation)   49

Chapter 4:   First Within Me
              (Christ-likeness)   61

Chapter 5:   Then Through Me
              (Christ-likeness 2)   85

Chapter 6:   My Heart As Yours
              (Prayer)   95

Chapter 7:   Your Words As Mine
              (Word)   113

Chapter 8:	Unleashed. Unstoppable. (Faith and Freedom)	125
Chapter 9:	I Will Trust Love (Intentional Relationship)	145
Chapter 10:	Away From The Lights Of The Stage (Lifestyle Ministry)	175
Conclusion:	Where True Beauty Is Displayed	189
Endnotes		199

Preface

Sometimes the heart
Feels more than words
Can find to voice
And in the wealth
Of emotion
The writer despairs
Of his choices

But ultimately
Between author
And reader
There is a trust
That the well intended
Will become the well-read:
The application of the words
The greater power
Than the writing of the same.

I have an insatiable need to be understood, more so than being liked. I can live with dislike (the fewer the people the better), but not with misunderstanding.

I will try to capture you with great stories, irritate you with frank opinions and engage you with vulnerable confessions. However, as much as I would like to condense everything into a single chapter, I have had to discipline myself to unfold the message, to hold certain convictions to a proper page, to risk that a reader would quit before the whole of the message can be conveyed.

You are God's artistry. As such, the transformation and effectiveness of the church is before us, and it will flow out of the change of our lives and the emphasis of our ministry. As a result of your reading and application, I want people to see natural relationships as their primary ministry, and I want churches to commit to transition from program-based and personality centered services to a people-equipping, community serving force.

He has made you able, and together we can do this.

By the way, Joseph is a writing band. Our writing may be the work of one or several, whatever the opportunity may call for, but it is written in the first person without attempt to distinguish the voice. We do so not to be secretive, but to downplay any one individual. It may end up to be an irrelevant practice, but for now we ask you to humor us.

Introduction

Maggie's father was her best friend. A 22 year veteran of the Air Force, he decided to settle into civilian life and move his family to Florida. As they drove him to the train station so that he could go prepare their new home, the car ran out of gas. Eleven year old Maggie watched as her father left the car and began to walk into town to a service station.

After what seemed an eternal wait, a stranger approached the car. What happened next devastated Maggie. The stranger informed them that her father was dead, the victim of a massive heart attack. The last she had ever seen of her father alive he was walking away, his back to her, growing smaller into the horizon until finally he was gone.

Maggie became both inconsolable and uncontrollable. Over the next several years she immersed herself in substance abuse and sex. By the age of 15 she became involved with a 27 year old man. By the age of 16 she gave birth to a baby boy. The father was abusive and chemically addicted, and Maggie had no choice but to leave and try to support the child on her own.

In her attempt to survive, Maggie hooked up with another older man. He, too, proved to be abusive, repeatedly beating her, threatening her family and forcing her into prostitution to support their drug habit.

One night, her boyfriend brought home another woman. Maggie, upset, told him she wanted out.

He pulled out a gun and said "Four bullets will get you out. You see that woman. In the morning I'm going to shoot her. Then I'm going to kill your boy. The last two bullets are for you and me."

ix

Maggie believed him. As he slept, she picked up the gun, placed the barrel to his head and pulled the trigger. She phoned the police, informed them of what she had done, and asked them to take care of her son.

Though charged with first-degree murder, she was allowed to plead guilty to manslaughter. She received a five-year suspended sentence and three years of probation.

By her own admission, she left the courtroom as empty as when she entered. After this, there was yet one more man, and one more threat to her life. This time she fled to her sister's place in North Carolina.

There she met Rich. He was in town for one night but stayed in her life for good. They married a year after they met. Rich's parents were Amish but Rich wasn't a practitioner of their faith. Their response to their son's tattooed, motorcycle bride was simple love.

Marriage wasn't easy for Maggie. Within a year Rich had moved out. A week later he gave her an ultimatum. He would move back if she and her son would go to church. Despite her reservations, she agreed.

In the back pew of a little country church Maggie met love. She met it in the people that welcomed her. She met it in her in-laws' constant love. And she met it in a Jesus she had never heard of before, not a God who took away her dad, but a Savior who claimed her as his own.

Both Maggie and Rich later applied to Bible College, and despite only having a ninth grade education, Maggie was accepted. Five years later she graduated with a double degree and magna cum laude.

God believes in you!

Mistake is setback, not elimination. The potential with which we were born is a canvas for God's unfailing love. In his hands, potential is always more promise than possibility.

Joseph

We live in a day when the promise of our life is underestimated. Too easily, circumstances, cultural expectations and criticism judge who we are and the effect we can have. Seemingly, we are one false step away from being voted off the island.

God does not underestimate us. He created us in his image. Of all that means, it certainly means this: People see God in us. The degree and clarity with which he is seen in us today is different than it will be in days that follow, but he is seen in us nonetheless.

After a beautiful and moving depiction in which the apostle Paul describes God's heart and intervention to save us, he declares, "For we are God's workmanship, created in Christ Jesus to do good works, which God prepared in advance for us to do."

The word workmanship is a great word. It is used only one other time in the New Testament where Paul writes "For since the creation of the world God's invisible qualities—his eternal power and divine nature—have been clearly seen, being understood from what has been made, so that men are without excuse." That phrase, "from what has been made" translates the word workmanship. Putting the two verses together, we understand that God makes himself known, both through creation and his re-creation in us.

The Greek word for workmanship is poiema, from which English derives its word poem. In other words, we are God's artistic expression, his rhyme in a world without reason. We are the song a person can't get out of their head. This can be a good thing.

God knows who we are and what we can be. His design is to show himself through us. He is seen in the process, not just the finished product. Today, whether we are degreed or still studying, retired or just beginning, the master or the apprentice, God is seen in us. And those with eyes to see will never be the same.

I used to draw. When I sketched, I didn't like people to see my work in progress. Now I write, and I still want people to wait until my effort is completed. I don't want them to see a project that needs work. Right or wrong, I believe people will judge me on the basis of the unfinished.

God is different. He invites people to see his work in progress. He wants people to see the details that might go unnoticed by the time the work is done. He wants to show the beauty of layers and mixes. God is not afraid of being judged on the basis of our unfinished life.

For too long, Christians have only wanted to show themselves after they've been cleaned up. We have assumed that a work in progress is a poor witness. Just the opposite has been experienced by those watching. We are labeled hypocrites because we profess what is true that is not—our completion. Genuineness, though, willingness for the details to be seen along the way, is part of God's artistry and appeal to people through us. That we are not yet finished, but growing, is a far more easier and honest witness to support.

We are God's delight and God's plan. Just as we are, and just as we are becoming. No vision, mission, strategy, ministry or program can replace God's first intent: To reveal himself through a people transforming. In a world where the genuine is too absent and where progress is too illusive, God chooses to demonstrate the art of change through sincere, simple believers as ourselves.

The regrets in our life
Cannot erase
His design for our life.

The Artist
Sees the imperfection
And instead of discarding
His work,
He mends,
He cleans.

Joseph

He draws out the potential
That drew him to us
In the first place.

What he saw
In his heart
He makes to see
With his eyes
So that, in the end
Beauty is on display.

Until we grasp this, we shortchange the gospel for gimmick. What people long for is replaced by what we think they expect. We judge outsiders to demand a perfect system flawlessly executed, when what they really want is hope: A loving God will accept them in their imperfections and give them strength, room and time to grow.

God not only believes in us as individuals, he believes in us together. God is in himself community, the relationship of Father, Son and Holy Spirit. Though Jesus would have died and risen just for me, he didn't. We all are objects of the cross. In relationship with each other, God reveals his self further still. Paul wrote "His intent was that now, through the church, the manifold wisdom of God should be made known . . ." The word manifold means "many varied". The full spectrum of God's wisdom is seen as we are in relationship together.

The common denominator to God's belief in us individually and his belief in us together is beauty. God makes one beautiful. God makes us beautiful.

Beauty is always the final description of God's work. God saw all that he had made and it was very good. Of the people Israel, he said, "And your fame spread among the nations on account of your beauty, because the splendor I had given you made your beauty perfect." The Bible calls us to "put on the Lord Jesus Christ" and promises that he will "present her to himself as a radiant church, without stain or wrinkle or any other blemish." And in the end, the final chapters of Revelation depict indescribable beauty.

Why is beauty God's desire? Because God attracts. We have many images of God, and the one image we emphasize least may be the one he cherishes most: He romances. He makes himself attractive to those who yet love him.

Come to me,
He whispers.

I am the beauty
That captures your eye;
The one who calls
To your best self
Through sunsets of splendor
And through simple delight.

I am the One
Who touches your heart
And turns despair
Into hope,
And your darkness
Into light.

There's a little gem of a verse that reads ". . . so that in every way they will make the teaching about God our Savior attractive. For the grace of God that brings salvation has appeared to all men. . . ." Paul wrote that to encourage Christians to live in such a way that God is attractive. Sometimes I live in a way that appears to make God . . . ugly.

Joseph

Nonetheless, God is working with me. He is working with me by working in me. He is making me beautiful. I need more than make-up; I need a miracle. And one of God's astounding truths is that he can reveal himself to another through me, as I am now, and as I am becoming. No amount of cover-up can accomplish that.

God loves people. He loves them enough he made them, saved them and wants to live eternally with them.

Certainly, God wants to be loved by people. He wants to be loved by people so much that he romances those who don't love him yet. He romances them through us. He's staked his whole dating plan on dressing up in human form. Before he leaves the house, he looks in the mirror to check himself and he sees you and me. He wants to hold their hand through ours, whisper to them through our breath, kiss them goodnight with our lips.

Eugene Peterson has said:

> Every Christian's story is a freedom story. Each tells how a person has been set free from the confines of small ideas, from the chains of what other people think, from the emotional cages of guilt and regret, from the prisons of self . . . We are free to change. The process of that change is always a good story, but is never a neat formula.

That's a life-saving quote for me. I grew up with a neat formula of faith that soured on me. Story has saved me. Freedom has breathed new life into me. We are in the process of change, in the story of being made into the image of the Son. His is a life worth becoming.

The question is: What does a life worth becoming look like? What is God making us to be today? When he is done, what will we look like? Along the way, what is he developing in us?

The answer may very well look different than our current experience.

Overview of the Book

People are living apart from God, and therefore, they are dying apart from God. It is a horrible reality.

In response, God has pursued those apart from him until it took him to the cross and from there to an empty grave and an expectant heaven. Part of his pursuit has involved demonstrating in individuals the change he can bring through his love, and demonstrating in his church the difference his love makes in our relationships. He shows off in us.

Consistently, though, God's people throughout history, first in the nation of Israel and again in his Church, have allowed a professional few to become the strength of the whole. As a result, God has been measured by the performance of the church's leadership, when all along he has wanted to be mirrored in the collective experience of both the weak and strong, the growing and the mature. When God's reputation is staked on leadership alone, then the pulpit is more valued than the pew, and image and reputation are more honored than lifestyle and genuineness.

We know this can no longer be. As God transitions his church back to grassroots strength, to the charisma of a collective experience, to the primacy of relationship, what can we anticipate?

The Bible demonstrates that God attracts through the beauty of a people who are characterized by grace, friendship and innovation. Grace fully experiences God. Friendship fully expresses God. Innovation, the willingness to do whatever it takes regardless of the cost, bridges the two.

This book is intended to coach us in how to experience all three. We are learning to become more like Christ so that we might give more of Christ away in natural, daily relationships God has entrusted to us. This is church. This is ministry. This is priority.

Grace, friendship and innovation are experienced as we cultivate personal transformation, intentional relationship and lifestyle
ministry. The leadership of the church must coach people in all
three of these arenas. As they do, we will transition the church from
program-based, personality-centered structures to movements of
relationships in which an individual pastors where they are.

You are his plan.

Fully Experiencing God

Grace is often treated as an object to be received rather than a
person to experience, namely God. Unintentionally, in an effort to
celebrate God's love in our life, we remove the focus from God himself. We sell the benefits of marriage while the bride remains veiled.

When this is so, the focus of grace is on what grace gives: Un-
conditional favor, unmerited love, etc. Grace does give these, but
first and foremost the focus of Biblical grace is on the giver before
the gifts.

The acronym for grace is true: God's Riches At Christ's Expense, but if we are not careful we focus on the *riches* and *expense*
rather than on *God* and *Christ*. Grace is about the person of God.
It is about experiencing his heart and inviting his character into
our heart. Grace is about God wanting us and us wanting God.

We need to reclaim the richness and texture of what it is to
"love God", a phrase that can lose its potency in over-use. It has become a motto, a bumper sticker, a mission statement, a clothing
line (okay, I don't know if the last one is true, but just wait).

Perhaps we begin to reclaim it by defining loving God as
wanting him, desiring him. I penned this in my journal at a time
when I was overwhelmed by pressure, but even more, greatly wanting Jesus.

xviii   A Life Worth Becoming

Set me free.
Free at last, once
And for all.
My regret,
Deep
Your redemption
Great.

Your Son in me,
Is my desire.
The draw of sin
Is an illusion,
A temporary want
That takes
More than it gives.

But not you.
You bring more
Than I imagine.
You out-give me,
Even when I give
My all and my best.

What is next?
I don't even ask.
Not yet.
For now, all I want
And seek
Is you.

I've heard it too: Love's not a feeling. Well, in part it is. To lose
sight of desire in love has left many Christians without feeling for

Joseph

xix

God. There are days God wants to take us by the hand, look us in the eye, and ask "yes, but do you want me?"

In our experience of God, we discover that he loves to give. These are the tangibles of grace, the gifts of the giver. He forgives and gives. He pardons and empowers.

We find a great account of this in Mark 2.

> A few days later, when Jesus again entered Capernaum, the people heard that he had come home. So many gathered that there was no room left, not even outside the door, and he preached the word to them. Some men came, bringing to him a paralytic, carried by four of them. Since they could not get him to Jesus because of the crowd, they made an opening in the roof above Jesus and, after digging through it, lowered the mat the paralyzed man was lying on. When Jesus saw their faith, he said to the paralytic, "Son, your sins are forgiven."
>
> Now some teachers of the law were sitting there, thinking to themselves, "Why does this fellow talk like that? He's blaspheming! Who can forgive sins but God alone?"
>
> Immediately Jesus knew in his spirit that this was what they were thinking in their hearts, and he said to them, "Why are you thinking these things? Which is easier: to say to the paralytic, 'Your sins are forgiven,' or to say, 'Get up, take your mat and walk'? But that you may know that the Son of Man has authority on earth to forgive sins. . . ." He said to the paralytic, "I tell you, get up, take your mat and go home." He got up, took his mat and walked out in full view of them all. This amazed everyone and they praised God, saying, "We have never seen anything like this!"

You can imagine being this paralytic. He's both excited and nervous. He's heard of Jesus and the miracles he can do. "Today", he thinks, "I might walk." As he nears, he sees the crowd. He's never been a fan of crowds. It's been a while since he looked strangers in the eye. It had been awhile since strangers had looked into his eyes.

xx   A Life Worth Becoming

"Perhaps", he now wonders, "this wasn't such a good idea." His friends persist though. Undaunted, they take off part of the roof.

Now in those days the house had a stairway on the outside leading to the roof, and the roof itself was constructed in sections. Still, in making an opening in the roof, clay, materials and dust would fall.

If you were the paralytic, are you nervous yet? You just interrupted the greatest teacher ever, got dust in his hair and managed to focus all eyes on you. What would you expect next?

Jesus ignores the dust and sees the man. Jesus forgives him. Then he enables him to walk. Why? This is who Jesus is: Grace is realized through him. He is love, and in his love he forgives and gives.

God is making us to be a people who act beyond expectation. A person expects judgment, criticism and rejection: They receive forgiveness. A person assumes we will see them as everyone else, from the waist down, but we hold their gaze and meet their need.

We are beautiful. God is attractive.

Fully Expressing God

A great part of Mark's story is the friends of the paralytic. Grace requires relationship for its expression. Jesus was a friend of sinners and called his disciples friends.

Friendship begins with God.

Again, in Mark 2 we read:

> Once again Jesus went out beside the lake. A large crowd came to him, and he began to teach them. As he walked along, he saw Levi son of Alphaeus sitting at the tax collector's booth. "Follow me," Jesus told him, and Levi got up and followed him.

"Me" is central to Jesus' invitation. We all follow someone or something. The Bible uses this word follow to describe how people

Joseph

chase after individuals, evil, ungodly desires, natural instincts and deceiving spirits. Jesus said the one to follow is him.

Jesus calls us to a person not a system. Sometimes following God seems more accurately described as following a set of expectations. Even when we say, "It's about relationship, not religion", we come to days we feel dry and realize that all those studies, classes and services became about the activity more than about God himself. Jesus wants to change this.

The word "follow" means *together along the way*. In other words, friendship with Jesus is about a process, not a formula. Remember Peterson's words, "The process of that change is always a good story but is never a neat formula."

I love the tale of the old preacher who declared, "The living Jesus is a problem in our religious institutions. Yes. Because if you are having a funeral, a nice funeral, and the dead person starts to move, there goes the funeral! And, dear brothers and sisters, Jesus is moving!"

When we have a friendship with God, one in which we are together along the way with Jesus, it defines the friendship we engage with others. As God is a friend to us, we are a friend to others. God, who emphasizes process over formula, models for us the room we give others, their journey we share with them.

That's why I love what happened with Levi. He chose to follow Jesus, and the next thing you know he throws a party for his friends.

> While Jesus was having dinner at Levi's house, many tax collectors and "sinners" were eating with him and his disciples, for there were many who followed him. When the teachers of the law who were Pharisees saw him eating with the "sinners" and tax collectors, they asked his disciples: "Why does he eat with tax collectors and 'sinners'?"
>
> On hearing this, Jesus said to them, "It is not the healthy who need a doctor, but the sick. I have not come to call the righteous, but sinners."

Levi was more concerned about changing himself than changing his friendships. He knew he could *bring change* to his friends without needing to *exchange* those friends for more sainted ones.

God wants us to pastor *where we are.* Pastor is a verb before it is ever a title. People, precious to God, have been entrusted to us. Some know God, some don't, but how we pastor them doesn't change. Funny, but I can pray for a non-believer even as I do a believer. Even more, if I'm not caught up in churchy, religious language, I can even tell my unbelieving friends how I've been praying for them. I haven't been rejected or stoned yet.

What does it look like to pastor where you are? Notice what the friends of the paralytic did. Though they couldn't do everything, they could do something. They could carry their friend to Jesus and get out of the way. *Something* is all God needs to work with. My friends don't need me to do everything. That is unrealistic. They also don't need me to do nothing. That is tragic. Something works just fine.

Also, they were willing to do whatever it takes. Risk the disfavor of the crowd? Not an issue when your friend could walk again. Replace a tile or two? Healing is worth the price.

When I was in high school my church had a door to door evangelism program I participated in. I remember one day in particular when I walked up to a door and knocked. As I waited for the owner to come to the door, I noticed a goose approaching me. The door opened, and just as I started my pitch the goose bit my leg and wouldn't let go. Here I am trying to witness and I'm getting goosed. Share the gospel and get bit by a goose? Conversion is worth it.

I love how the text says that Jesus saw their faith. How do you see faith? Obviously, he saw the act produced by faith. He saw their willingness to do whatever it takes so that Jesus could do what only he can do. And he sees our faith. He sees how we give to another, simply, without notice. But he notices. The church of the future, the beautiful church, will be characterized by life-changing friendship. A life worth becoming serves the heart of another, not necessarily the stage of the crowds.

Gifts Wed To Opportunity

Innovation bridges grace and friendship. In expressing the God I experience, I do whatever it takes regardless of the cost. Innovation is where my gift is met with opportunity. I'm not concerned if it's never been done before, and I'm especially not concerned if someone says "we don't do it that way".

The disciples of Jesus once ate by picking grain on the Sabbath. The Pharisees criticized him and he reminded them that the Sabbath was made for man, not man for the Sabbath. Jesus understood the times, and he was willing to pay the price for his conviction.

A life worth becoming sees the need and meets it, whether it's been done before or not, whether it is socially acceptable or finally radical. Cost is not a consideration. Recognizing a new day is.

How I Got Here

On occasion a person will say something unforgettable. It happened to me when a friend at the time described our current generation of leadership as the third leg of the relay. The image has never left me.

The purpose of the third leg is to set up the fourth leg for victory. I am called to prepare my children and grandchildren to grab the baton, finish strong and cross the finish line.

The image took hold when I was at dinner with a group of pastors who provided leadership to church planters for their denomination. At the time I was pastor of a very large church in Southern California, and I helped coordinate these leaders' efforts. We were talking about our denomination's goal to plant so many churches by a certain time frame.

I spoke up. I didn't plan it, but I said something like this:

> But what do we mean by churches. If we mean a certain amount of people inhabiting a facility and conducting services as we do today, then forget it. The church of the future will be wrapped around natural networks of relationship. There is a person working in this restaurant right now who loves Jesus. They need to see their self as a pastor right here, shepherding saved and unsaved friends and workers God has entrusted to them. We need to equip people to pastor naturally, to "do church" in Starbucks, in the restaurant after work, in their own home. We have to move the church away from program based, personality centered ministry and redefine ministry by what happens with people through people everyday. We have to get to a place where the person in the pew doesn't feel guilty that they aren't serving God by volunteering in the church's programs, when they are serving God everyday in their workplace, home and neighborhood.

I think we all agreed, caught a movie after dinner and then went back to our churches to do business as usual. But I knew God had caught my attention.

My own background will spill out over the course of the following pages. Suffice it to say that when I was five years old I was the first in my family to come to faith in Christ. I started preaching when I was sixteen. I planted churches, coached leaders, and led a mega-church, whatever that means.

And I was deeply troubled. I had everything I had ever prayed for in terms of ministry, only to realize I'd been praying for the wrong thing. Okay, I prayed for right things, but I expected the results to be different than they were. Has that ever happened to you?

Joseph

Have you ever thought if you just "had that" or "accomplished this" something would be true only to find out otherwise?

I was Bible believing, Spirit filled and purpose driven.

And I had lost sight of people.

This book is intended to encourage us and to equip us to become more like Jesus Christ and to pastor where we are, to bring relational influence through lifestyle ministry. A life worth becoming is God's friend and a good friend.

God values church leadership. We are right to honor those who lead among us. Our times together for worship, instruction and ministry are irreplaceable. But the strength of the church's ministry is you. It is you in your relationships. It is you in your every day. This book is about God through you.

The first three chapters devote themselves to a closer look at grace, friendship and innovation. The rest of the chapters describe how to develop and express those traits through cultivating Christlikeness, intentional relationship and lifestyle ministry.

When finished, we will have been called to realize that as individuals there is no more effective ministry than being like Jesus in the life of those we love, and that as the church we must place greater emphasis on relationship and lifestyle than on leadership and show.

It is time.
Time to stand
With sure feet
And singular mind;
Time to speak
With whole heart
In full allegiance
To the One we love.

A Life Worth Becoming

We will be a fellowship
Of the unashamed
Not the unassuming.
We will be a fellowship
Of the undeterred
Not of the uncommitted.

We are his.
Simply. Daily.
Becoming,
Not yet arrived.

We are theirs.
Open. Genuine.
Involved,
Not removed.

We will not hold out
But will be sold out,
We will not hold back
But we will give back.

Our song
Will not be silenced,
Our speech
Will not be stilled.

God is in us.
Sin could not stain him.
Man could not constrain him.
Death could not hold him and
Satan could not overcome him.

Joseph   xxvii

We will not hide him.

It is time:
Time to wake up, sit up, get up and move up.

We will not whine over pettiness.
We will not dine with compromise.

It is time
To embrace love over hurt,
Forgiveness over failure,
Quiet over gossip,
Honesty over manipulation
And obedience over convenience.

We will not pretend
To have it made
When the God of grace
Is making us still.

We will not demand that
Those who do not
Know him yet
Act as if they do.
We will be with them
Along the way.

We will do
Whatever it takes
Regardless of the cost
For God's creative hand
Will not be cuffed

By the critic
Whose days have passed.

In all,
Hearts that have longed for him
Will find him.
Lives that have sought him will
Be like him.

Beauty will be ours
And they will be his.

I Want You

My friend, Steve, mentors people around the world in what it means to follow Christ. They range from names you would recognize to high school students. He is as likely to be praying with people on a football field as he is a politician's office.

Recently he met with a group of captains of a college football team. They had just buried one of their teammates.

He played for them a scene from the movie Gladiator. In the movie, Maximus, a former general enslaved as a gladiator, looks for revenge upon Commodus, who had recently become emperor after murdering his father, Marcus Aurelius. Maximus has just won a great victory in the arena and the emperor, who does not know the gladiator is the famed general, approaches to meet him. He asks his name.

> Maximus replies, "My name is gladiator". He then turns around and begins to walk away.
>
> Commodus calls out, "How dare you show your back to me, slave. You will remove your helmet and tell me your name."
>
> Maximus stops, takes a deep breath, removes his helmet and turns to face Commodus.
>
> Maximus declares, "My name is Maximus Decimus Meridius. Commander of the armies of the North, general of the Felix legions, loyal servant to the true emperor Marcus Aurelius. Father to a murdered son, husband to a murdered wife, and I will have my vengeance in this life or the next."

At the end of the clip, Steve pulls out a simple, silver engraved key chain. He shows them one side that has his name engraved. Then he shows them the other side. Engraved there is the number 14.

Steve says, "Now you guys know I didn't have the physique to wear this number (a quarterback's number, which Steve was not). So why number 14? Because when the Titanic sank, and 16 lifeboats deployed, many of which were not filled to capacity and had plenty of room for more people to board for safety, Lifeboat 14 was only one of two to return and pull victims from the water."

"You have to know who you are", he continues. "Every day I see this number and remember that I too was rescued, and that I am surrounded by people needing to be rescued too."

Steve proceeded to hand each of them an engraved key chain, their name on one side and number 14 engraved on the other.

God has a key chain for each of us. On one side is engraved our name. On the other side is engraved "grace".

For years, I failed to recognize grace fully. I knew the role of grace in salvation, but failed to apply it in my relationship with Christ and others. I praised God for the amazing grace that saved me, and patted myself on the back for the effort I made not to need much of it again.

A few years ago the Lord invited me on a journey in which grace was to be my companion. I came to know her in ways never before, and grew in my love for her.

Grace is the definitive trait of beauty. The beauty he is working within us and his church is the grace that experiences him and then expresses it to others.

Again, grace is not about something we receive but about a person we experience. Love from God begins with God himself. His heart for us and his character toward us is the source of every expression of grace. I love the gifts grace gives. I love the giver first.

But Do You Want Me?

Why is the distinction between giver and gift so important?

I remember a story line from Everybody Loves Raymond where they flashback to the day Ray proposed to his wife, Deborah.

Joseph

Ray had published his first sports article in the paper, and in the article he proposed to Deborah. Just as she began to read the article, Ray's dad enters the room, interrupts their time and grabs the newspaper. Proud of his son's accomplishment, he reads the article out loud despite Ray's protests, and ends up proposing on Ray's behalf. Later, Ray's brother points out that Deborah didn't really say "yes" to him: She said yes to his mom in the excitement of the moment. Alone with Deborah he confesses his concern, wondering if she's sure she wants to marry him. He turns so that he is in profile to her, his large nose protruding from his face.

Obviously, God isn't insecure. He isn't asking from heaven "Are you sure you want me? I can be unpredictable, you know? I like to get my way. I'm easily misunderstood and not everybody likes me."

Sometimes, though, I wonder if God doesn't want to interrupt all of our activities—all that we do in his name and for the sake of mission—and ask, "But do you want me?"

He knows I am easily distracted. I remember as a young Associate Pastor of tiring after a couple of years work. Ministry seemed comprised of meetings, organization, urgent-staffing and conflict resolution. I took a day off and was wandering around the park, reading and praying. I felt dry. I thought "this isn't what I signed up for". I wanted God back.

Have you experienced those times? I worked through the episode, and you have worked through yours. But we recall what it is to so give ourselves to activity that we lose touch with our first love. We know what it is to seek God's hand that we miss his heart.

Instead, God is beautifying a people who are marked by passionate, relentless love for him, a love that is defined as desire and want as well as obedience and trust. A life worth becoming craves to see him, hear him, and invite him in.

We personify the words of Anne Cousin who wrote "The bride eyes not her garment, but her dear bridegroom's face. I will

4   A Life Worth Becoming

not gaze at glory but on my King of grace. Not at the crown He gives but on His pierced hand; the lamb is all the glory of Emmanuel's land."

And as we experience him, we give him away. The Bible teaches that Jesus is full of grace and truth, and that grace and truth are realized through him. To realize grace and truth doesn't mean we just receive it. It transforms us so that it is realized by others through us as well. Beauty reflects Jesus. We experience him, and all he has to give by grace, so that we might allow others to experience us, and all we have to give by his grace.

So how do we experience grace, and how do we express grace?

Experiencing Grace

A Biblical study of grace reveals that God saves us to himself for a relationship in which he forgives and gives.

Each of these aspects, his *presence with us,* his *pardon of us* and his *power for us* offer shades of meaning of what it is to fully experience God and to be transformed by grace.

Paul wrote "But because of his great love for us, God, who is rich in mercy, made us alive with Christ even when we were dead in transgressions—it is by grace you have been saved."

Grace is the active agent in our salvation. But what does it mean to be saved? The verse defines it for us: We are made "alive with Christ." This is the first of three verbs prefixed by the Greek word *syn* meaning "with": We were made alive with him, raised with him, and seated with him. The emphasis is on the "with".

Remember Adam? He was formed by God, made in his image. They were tight. And then is recorded for us one of the saddest verses of all: "The man and his wife heard the sound of the Lord God as he was walking in the garden in the cool of the day,

Joseph   **5**

and they hid from the Lord God." And God, who rejoiced in the making of man, uttered the words whose echo was the sound of impending darkness: "Where are you?"

It was the second worst day of God's life.

We, too, know what it is to hide. We try to cover up our sin and make up for our error. And when we fall short, we avoid God. We hide behind our schedule, bury ourselves in work, and surround ourselves with the crowd.

Salvation, grace realized, erases the sin, redeems the errors and removes the barriers. We are once again his. We are with him. Grace is not realized *apart* from him. It is why of all the images of the church in the New Testament—body, building, temple to name a few—the final image is the lasting image: "The Spirit and the bride say 'come'".

Bride is God's favorite motif for his people. He is romantic. He loves to be with his bride. Can you imagine God writing this to you?

> I want you to see me
> From across the room
> And allow the look of my eyes
> To signal a desire too great
> For words.
>
> I want each step we take
> Towards each other
> To dance to the hastening
> Beat of our heart
>
> And I want our outstretched
> Hands to touch,
> And in that touch
> For our spirits to soar

A Life Worth Becoming

In the embrace that follows,
The perfect fit of two
Pressed as one and
Yearning for more,
I want both passion
And peace
To flow from head to toe

For the first time
In your life
I want questions
To be left
Without answers
Until the answers
Present themselves
In the natural course
Of their day

I want to lead you to our room
To close the door to an outside world
And draw you to me
The walls growing silent
Knowing they are about to store
Forever hence
The sounds of lovers released
And at play.

We rest, and you know
That in this time and place
I have met you on bended knee
Pledged myself fully and daily,
To cherish each moment we share
As a gift of endless grace.

But What Does It Mean

If we emphasize the gifts over the giver, we short-change salvation. What we *save* people with is what we *save* people to: And if all we do in our message of the gospel is focus on the benefits, we save people to the benefits.

When this happens, prayer deteriorates and becomes mostly about requests. Ministry is planned and then prayed about rather than prayed about and planned. Worship services are evaluated by the public's experience—God is apparently content that people were just willing to attend.

God loves us so much. He wants our prayer to be partnership, our ministry to be adventure, and our worship to be an outpouring of Him. He doesn't care if our words aren't perfect, our plans aren't brilliant and our voice is out of tune.

He loves us so much he saved us to be with him.

Paul teaches "For all have sinned and fall short of the glory of God, and are justified freely by his grace through the redemption that came by Christ Jesus. God presented him as a sacrifice of atonement, through faith in his blood. He did this to demonstrate his justice, because in his forbearance he had left the sins committed beforehand unpunished."

The word justified is a legal term. It means we are made acceptable to God. The word redemption is borrowed from the marketplace, defined as to be bought with a price (think of a slave being purchased and then set free). The word atonement is a relational term and speaks of harmony and unity.

God piles on the imagery to declare that in any and every situation he wants us to himself. No wonder that a few verses later Paul writes "since we have been justified through faith, we have peace with God through our Lord Jesus Christ, through whom we have gained access by faith into this grace in which we now stand." Say it with me: God wants us with him.

8   A Life Worth Becoming

One of my worst moments as a parent occurred when my oldest daughter, all of about nine years old, was playing on a basketball team and the rest of the family was there to watch. I was helping coach. I can get a little intense when I coach. In this particular game, our undefeated streak was on the line as the other team was playing nasty and aggressive (at least, that's how I saw it). Towards the end of the game, I felt a tug on my pants and heard my youngest daughter asking for me. I turned and said "Not now!"

I knew when the words escaped me that I had just suffered a really bad dad moment. I found my youngest daughter, looked her in the eye, asked her to forgive me and assured her that any time was the right time for her and me. Gratefully, she forgave me and I've had opportunities to do better since.

Our Father never says "Not now." Now is always good.

Rose Hartwick Thorpe writes of a soldier who was condemned to die by execution at a ringing of a curfew bell. The soldier was engaged to be married to a beautiful young girl named Bessie. As the sexton prepared to pull the rope to ring the bell, Bessie climbed to the top of the belfry, reached out and held on to the tongue of the huge bell at the risk of her life. The sexton rang it and she was smashed against the sides of the bell but the bell was silent. Once the bell ceased to swing, Bessie descended from the tower. When General Cromwell approached, Bessie confessed:

> At his feet she told her story,
> Showed her hands all bruised and torn;
> And her sweet young face, still haggard
> With the anguish it had worn;
> Touched his heart with sudden pity,
> Lit his eyes with misty light:
> "Go, your lover lives," said Cromwell,
> "Curfew will not ring tonight."

Wide they flung the massive portals, led the prisoner forth to die
All his bright young life before him, 'Neath the darkening
    English sky.
Bessie came, with flying footsteps, eyes aglow with
    lovelight sweet;
Kneeling on the turf beside him, laid his pardon at his feet.
In his brave, strong arms he clasped her, kissed the face
    upturned and white
Whispered, Darling, you have saved me, curfew will not
    ring tonight."

Paul also wrote, "I do not set aside the grace of God."

How do we set aside the grace of God? According to the rest of this verse, we set aside God's grace when we seek to accomplish through law what God has already accomplished in Christ. We try to achieve by our own works what God achieved in his.

That's called living apart from God, not with God. Paul put it this way "After beginning with the Spirit, are you now trying to attain your goal by human effort?"

One more time: God wants us with him. A life worth becoming begins with grace, the inseparable bond of his heart and ours.

Eugene Peterson's description of David touched me deeply. He wrote, "The single most characteristic thing about David is God. David believed in God, thought about God, imagined God, addressed God, prayed to God. The largest part of David's existence wasn't David, but God."

That's what I'm talking about.

Forgiven

God's heart is to forgive. To experience God is to receive his forgiveness. Forgiveness is the taste of grace.

A Life Worth Becoming

Remember our friend the paralytic in Mark 2. Jesus said to him "Son, your sins are forgiven." In calling him son he reminded him of his relationship. In naming it "your sins" he reminded him of his responsibility. Essentially, Jesus was saying the sin, for which you are fully responsible and has caused you to live apart from God, is removed from you that you might you might live again in relationship with the Father.

Before Jesus ever healed him, he forgave him. Why? Because forgiveness remains man's greatest need.

God forgives us that we might be restored to him and realize Christ-likeness in our life. Unforgiven, we live apart from God and untrue to our self. Forgiven, we both belong and become.

Return with me to Adam. He has sinned. He and Eve made coverings for themselves and then they hid. This is the behavior of shame.

Shame is a judgment we make of our belonging, worth and competence. Bound in shame, I believe that if one really knew me they would reject me. So I cover myself. In his book, False Intimacy, Harry Schaumbers writes:

> Illegitimate shame is present when we desperately want to be viewed as sufficient, to be loved and accepted in relationships, and yet we move away from genuine intimacy to avoid being known as someone who isn't perfect. Illegitimate shame can make us fear that something harmful will happen to us, that what we hope for in relationships we won't ever be able to experience.

Further, captive to shame, I believe that in the end God will banish me. So I hide. I hide by drowning myself in sin or by dressing myself in religious devotion. Either way, I silence the word of God. Loud parties or loud prayers can both drown out his voice.

Into this shame, Jesus speaks "Son, your sins are forgiven." Forgiveness not only exposes the sin but expresses God's heart.

Joseph

Brennan Manning has written "The heart of Jesus loves us as we are and not as we should be, beyond worthiness and unworthiness, beyond fidelity and infidelity; He who loves us in the morning sun and the evening rain without caution, regret, boundary, limit, or breaking point."

God forgives us to restore us to relationship with him.

Max Lucado writes:

> He humbled himself. He went from commanding angels to sleeping in the straw. From holding stars to clutching Mary's finger. The palm that held the universe took the nail of a soldier. Why? Because that's what love does. It puts the beloved before itself. Your soul was more important than his blood. Your eternal life was more important to him than his place in heaven, so he gave up his so you could have yours.

God also forgives us to renew us. Forgiveness is the avenue to Christ-likeness. When God redeemed us, he settled once for all the judgment of our belonging, worth and competence. He chose me, so I belong. He bought me with the blood of his Son, so I am invaluable. He has made me competent as a son.

Sin makes us less but forgiveness makes us more.

Emily Dickinson captured sin's destruction when she penned:

> Crumbling is not an instant's act,
> A fundamental pause;
> Dilapidation's processes
> Are organized decays.
>
> Tis first a cobweb on the soul,
> A cuticle of dust,
> A borer in the axis,
> An elemental rust.

A Life Worth Becoming

Ruin is formal, devil's work,
Consecutive and slow—
Fail in an instant no man did,
Slipping is crash's law.

During some uniquely dark days, I wrote the following in my journal:

I can no longer feel.
Unsure of anything
I do not even know
How to define myself.

And, so,
The thoughts that come my way
I know not if they belong,
If they should go
Or if they should stay.

I am numb
To all
But despair.

I have fought
Friend and foe
Until I am exhausted
Alone from the one and
Vulnerable to the other.

Where did I go?
How did I get here?
I am unraveled.

Joseph

With pressure this great
The only emotion
I can feel
Is relief.

But then
Day dawns.
Light upon
A resurrection morning
It is not relief, but
Rebirth.

No one can
Orchestrate this.
It is you.
You alone
Stand in the midst
Of the flames
And deliver.

You alone
Pierce the darkness
And shine upon
Your unbreakable claim.

Claim me.

I need never question what God is doing in my life. I know the answer: He is making me like Jesus. The Bible says that in all things God works for the good of those who love him and are called

A Life Worth Becoming

according to his purpose. And what is that purpose: "To be conformed to the likeness of his Son." Because of this, Paul affirms:

- If God is for us, who can be against us.
- Who will bring any charge against those whom God has chosen?
- Who is he that condemns? Christ Jesus, who died—more than that who was raised to life—is at the right hand of God and is also interceding for us.
- Who shall separate us from the love of Christ?

When I resigned as Senior Pastor of a large church and entered into an undefined season, I told my mentor "I don't know a lot about what is ahead, but I do know this—God will use this to make me more like his Son." Whatever situation you find yourself in, your conviction can be the same. God uses victory and defeat, hope and heartbreak, storm and stillness all for one end: To make you like Jesus. His is the life worth becoming.

In forgiveness, specifically, God restores us and renews us. It is a process born from relationship, not perfected within a system. Grace is God himself present with us, his Spirit working in us. He doesn't quit. He didn't come in, see the room a mess, and flip on the vacancy sign as he left. He checked in to stay.

Given

God not only forgives, he gives. He said to the paralytic "Get up, take your mat and go home." The text says, "He got up, took his mat and walked out in full view of them all. This amazed everyone and they praised God, saying "We have never seen anything like this!"

Man's point of need is God's place of courtship. Jesus loved to ask, "What do you want me to do for you?" Grace gives—so much so that the Greek word for grace and gift is the same.

The Bible shows that by his grace God gives both power and provision.

I've Got The Power

From the New Testament perspective, power is both an inward and outward working.

Inwardly, God's power strengthens us to persevere and to persist. Paul said "I pray that out of his glorious riches he may strengthen you with power through his Spirit in your inner being." Previously, he had prayed in that they would know God's "incomparably great power for us who believe. That power is like the working of his mighty strength."

In these verses Paul stacks up the imagery. The word *power,* described as incomparably great, means an explosive strength. The word *working* is energy, and pictures someone straining to the point of breaking sweat. The word *mighty* depicts something that is extremely effective in accomplishing its goal, and the word *strength* was used for the image of a very strong man.

The promise for the Christian is that God's power is at work in them. As a result, we don't give up when others would quit, and we don't give in when others would compromise.

When we feel weak, we draw near. The apostle James wrote "But he gives more grace. That is why the Scripture says 'God opposes the proud but gives grace to the humble." In a classic verse,

A Life Worth Becoming

Paul quotes the Lord saying to him "My grace is sufficient for you, for my power is made perfect in weakness."

One of the most moving stories I've ever heard was about a girl named Nikki. Her testimony is told in *A Second Helping of Chicken Soup for the Soul*.

In seventh grade Nikki was diagnosed with leukemia. Chemotherapy was necessary, and Nikki suffered the loss of her hair. For a seventh grade girl, few things feel worse than losing your hair.

During the summer she bought a wig. Upon returning to school for eighth grade, kids teased her despite her popularity. They would pull off her wig, and she would bend down, pick it up, and wipe away the tears as she headed to class.

Finally, she had enough and told her parents she couldn't do it anymore. For Nikki there was nothing more hurtful than rejection by her friends. She would walk the halls, and the crowds would part. She would enter the cafeteria and students would leave. Working through hair loss was one thing, and facing the possibility of eternity was another, but to lose her friends was hardest of all. Nikki's parents told her she could stay home if she wished.

Over the weekend, though, she heard about two boys. One was a seventh-grader in Arkansas who took his Bible to school with him. When he was confronted by three boys, he handed the Bible to one of them and challenged him if he had enough courage to carry it around for even one day.

The second story was about a sixth-grader named Jimmy Masterdino. He wanted Ohio to have a state motto. He thought up the words, organized the petitions and took it before the State Legislature. Because of his effort, the state motto for Ohio is "With God, all things are possible."

That next Monday, Nikki put on her wig and told her parents she was going back to school. They drove her there, and she

Joseph

hugged and kissed them before getting out of the car. Then she looked at them.

> She said, "Today I'm going to find out who my best friend is. Today I'm going to find out who my real friends are." And with that she grabbed her wig off her head and she set it on the seat beside her. She said, "They take me for who I am Daddy, or they don't take me at all. I don't have much time left. I've got to find out who they are today." She started to walk, took two steps, then turned and said, "Pray for me." They said, "We are, baby." And as she walked toward 600 kids, she heard her dad say, "That's my girl,"
>
> A miracle happened that day. She walked through that playground, into that school, and not one loud mouth or bully, no one, made fun of the little girl with all the courage.
>
> Nikki has taught thousands of people that to be yourself, to use your own God-given talent, and stand up for what is right even in the midst of uncertainty, pain, fear and persecution is the only true way to live.

God's power within us strengthens us so that we do not give up and we do not give in. We persevere. We persist.

God's power also enables us to do the supernatural.

In the book of Acts we read "Now Stephen, a man full of God's grace and power, did great wonders and miraculous signs among the people." And "Paul and Barnabas spent considerable time there, speaking boldly for the Lord, who confirmed the message of his grace by enabling them to do miraculous signs and wonders."

I know: "That was them back then". But we are too quick to disqualify ourselves.

The whole idea behind prayer and spiritual gifts is power not our own at work through us and into the life of another. Both prayer and spiritual gifts receive fuller treatment in chapters ahead, but for now consider this. Our experience of God is both *in* and through. The Bible says we pray in the Spirit. Spiritual gifts are manifestations of the Spirit. He who dwells in us authors our prayer and our performance.

I had the privilege of first preaching publicly just shy of my 16th birthday. I was involved in a large, fast-growing church, and they gave priority to mentoring and discipleship. As a result, they occasionally held a youth night where teens participated in the service. Two of us were asked to share the preaching time, but a week before the service my friend broke his foot and opted out of the opportunity. I was asked to fill the preaching time. I prayed a lot before that night. Several hundred people showed up, and when it was time, I approached the pulpit and stood there, dressed in a borrowed sport coat slightly too large for me. At least my clip-on tie matched the shirt and coat.

I preached. I was young, nervous and a bit silly looking. Yet, I still refer to it as my best preaching ever, because one week later as I was at church getting ready for choir practice my dad phoned. He asked me to come home. When I got there, my oldest brother was there as well. He was older by twelve years and a former Marine. He was a heavyweight boxer in the Corps. I looked even sillier when I used to wear his boxing robe he gave me. Dad explained that as a result of the service the week before my brother had placed faith in Christ as Savior. We prayed together in one of the more tender times I remember as a family.

The Spirit uses who he chooses, even a kid in borrowed clothes speaking on borrowed time.

By God's grace you are strong. For too long we have associated strength of ministry with public performance. And may those with public gifts excel. But real strength is demonstrated in the trenches, where the practical power of grace meets the grit of a typical day.

People are looking to see if God makes a difference. It is one thing to hear it. It is another to see it. And it is seen in you—not perfectly, but enough to inspire hope and possibility.

The life worth becoming realizes a strength that doesn't give up and doesn't give in. It believes that by God's power anything is possible at any time in any place.

The Lord Is My Shepherd. . . .

Romans 8:32 promises "He who did not spare his own Son, but gave him up for us all—how will he not also, along with him—graciously give us all things."

We find in God not only the power we require but every provision we need. The promise is reiterated throughout Scripture, from David declaring "The Lord is my Shepherd, I shall not be in want,"—to Jesus promising "all these things will be given to you—to Paul's reassurance "And my God will meet all your needs according to his glorious riches in Christ Jesus."

God provides. "If you then, though you are evil," Jesus said, "know how to give good gifts to your children, how much more will your Father in heaven give good gifts to those who ask him."

I have a bad habit that doesn't serve me well. Several years ago, my wife and I were interviewing a young married couple for a position with our ministry. They had invited us to their house for dinner. The food was good, though simple on their limited budget, and afterwards they served ice cream. I love ice cream! This particular ice cream was a low-end brand, but chocolate sauce makes anything taste fine, and I was quite happy.

After the dishes were cleared, I was standing in the kitchen. I opened the refrigerator to look. I can't help myself. A closed refrigerator is an open invitation. If the Lord had spoken to me in the Garden of Eden "But of this refrigerator you shall not open", I doubt the story would have ended any better than it did for Adam. So I scanned the shelves, closed the door and opened the freezer section on top. There before me was the cheap ice cream. But what did I see tucked behind it? Expensive brand ice cream! I couldn't stop my mouth in time. I shouted, "Hey, you hid the good stuff."

The young bride was horrified. Her husband was hired.

God doesn't hide the good stuff. He gives of himself, and therefore he gives the best.

Expressing Grace

God wants his church, the beautiful bride, to be known for grace. Grace, before anything else, is about experiencing the person of Jesus Christ. In his grace, he forgives and gives, meeting our needs for his presence, power and provision.

If we are to be characterized by grace, then people will experience in relationship with us the person of Jesus Christ. He will be present with them through us. He will forgive through us. He will give to them through us.

We give Jesus. Before we ever sell the benefits of salvation (come on, I used to go door to door), we present him in such a way that people love him.

This is the incredible truth: God, awesome, holy and incomparable, indwells you that he might show himself through you. "You show that you are a letter from Christ", Paul wrote, "written not with ink but with the Spirit of the living God, not on tablets of stone but on tablets of human hearts."

Radical Forgiveness

Several years ago I was on a team ministering in Murmansk, Russia. Murmansk is located off the Arctic Circle. We were the first

Joseph

American team allowed into some of their schools, and in particular a maximum security prison.

We were led into the assembly room of the prison where we were scheduled to hold an evangelistic service. The room was dark, and I was surprised that the walls were painted with murals depicting military violence. I expected calm ponds and soft classical music. On either side of me were armed guards—until they let the prisoners in. Several hundred violent-offenders came into the room, and as I looked around there wasn't a guard to be seen. I looked at my translator awaiting reassurance, received none, half-smiled and began the service.

At the end, I don't know how many came forward to embrace Christ as their Savior. It was a lot. The room was filled with energy. One man approached me. He began to speak, and my friend translated, "I am in here because I killed eight people. Can God forgive me too?"

What would you have said?

If forgiveness remains man's greatest need, then communicating forgiveness is our greatest ministry.

Paul wrote "Be kind and compassionate to one another, forgiving each other, just as in Christ God forgave you."

How did he forgive us?

> "He forgave us all our sins, having canceled the written code, with its regulations, that was against us and that stood opposed to us; he took it away, nailing it to the cross. And having disarmed the powers and authorities, he made a public spectacle of them, triumphing over them by the cross."

The idea behind the word disarmed is to strip to complete nakedness. He made a spectacle of them, which is a word meaning to display. Classical writings used the same word to speak of displaying the spoils of war. Such a display was public, suggesting openness and confidence. The word triumph was used of the emperor's victorious parade upon returning home from defeating the enemy in their land.

In other words, Jesus forgave our sins at the price of his blood, and he stripped the enemy of any means of retaliation. Salvation is complete. He forgave us and he freed us.

Jesus died to pay a debt we couldn't afford, and rose that we might live a life we could not live. God has entrusted to us precious people who need to know that no sin is outside the touch of God's grace. They need to know that no promise of their life is so broken that God's power can't not reclaim, renew, rebuild and restore. They will know this through relationship with us. They will know this because we forgive.

Why does God call us to forgive? Because when I forgive someone, it opens the possibility to them that if I can forgive, perhaps God will forgive. They don't understand at the time that my forgiveness is a result of his grace in my life. What they do understand is that where others would hold a grudge, strike back or walk away, I offer continued relationship. And somewhere along the line, they pick up that I not only love them but I love God, and maybe the two have something to do with each other.

I attended a seminar held by Lee Strobel in which he told of his own friendship with a woman who was investigating the claims of Christ. During their friendship she wrote this poem:

Do you know
Do you understand
That you represent
Jesus to me?

Do you know
Do you understand
That when you

Joseph

Treat me with gentleness,
It raises the question in my mind
That maybe He is gentle, too.
Maybe He isn't someone
Who laughs when I am hurt.

Do you know
Do you understand
That when you listen to my questions
And you don't laugh,
I think, "What if Jesus is interested in me, too?"

Do you know
Do you understand
That when I hear you talk about arguments and conflict
        and scars from your past
That I think, "maybe *I am* just a regular person
Instead of a bad, no good little girl who deserves abuse."

If you care,
I think maybe He cares—
And then there's this flame of hope
That burns inside of me
And for a while
I am afraid to breathe
Because it might go out.

Do you know
Do you understand
That your words are His words?
Your face, His face
To someone like me?

Please be who you say you are.
Please, God, don't let this be another trick.
Please let this be real.
Please.

Surprising Gifts

Those who love God, who are being made beautiful by him, will be generous givers. They will surprise people with their gifts. Such givers understand that generosity is an end run around people's defenses. It can catch a person off-guard, set them to asking questions, and motivate their own generosity.

And when givers recognize that they simply partner with God, and realize that God is giving to another through them, they understand generous giving costs them nothing. We give what we first receive. It only costs us if we hang on to it.

Am I being naïve? Remember what Paul wrote:

> "Entirely on their own, they pleaded with us for the privilege of sharing in this service to the saints. And they did not do as we expected, but they gave themselves first to the Lord and then to us in keeping with God's will . . . And God is able to make all grace abound to you, so that in all things at all times, having all that you need, you will abound in every good work . . . For you know the grace of our Lord Jesus Christ, that though he was rich, yet for your sakes he became poor, so that you through his poverty might become rich."

They got it. God provides. We give. Not as an act of obedience, nor a religious rite, nor a spiritual investment plan (phone now!). We give because we share in God's love for people, and what we have to give has been intended to pass through us.

Joseph   25

The New Testament paints a portrait in which we give in three ways. First, we receive power to give power.

Spiritual gifts have been misrepresented. For something so amazingly beautiful, they have become the subject and source of debate and division. Sounds a bit like Satan, doesn't it?

The Bible defines spiritual gifts for itself. Paul writes "Now to each one the manifestation of the Spirit is given for the common good." What is a spiritual gift? It is the manifestation of the Spirit. It is God wanting to give something to someone through you. Not very complicated, is it?

The previous verse reads, "There are different kinds of workings, but the same God works all of them in all men." We saw the word work before when discussing God's power. It is the idea of straining. God breaks a sweat through you to give into the life of another.

We see this in action:

> "With great power the apostles continued to testify to the resurrection of the Lord Jesus, and much grace was upon them all."
> "I will not venture to speak of anything except what Christ has accomplished through me in leading the Gentiles to obey God by what I have said and done—by the power of signs and miracles, through the power of the Spirit.

At this stage someone will step in and say "But those were the apostles. Gifts died. . . . not all, just those cool ones where hurting people actually got healed, confused people actually got clarity from God and demonic powers got their butts kicked."

And I will say, "That is a tired argument gathering dust in a theological closet no one cares to open." Patiently, I will open my Bible to I Peter 4:10–11. There I will read: "Each one should use whatever gift he has received to serve others, *faithfully administering God's grace in its various forms.* If anyone speaks, he should do

26 A Life Worth Becoming

it as one speaking the very words of God. If anyone serves, he should do it with the strength God provides, *so that in all things God may be praised through Jesus Christ.*

I will couple that verse with I Corinthians 12:11 "All these are the work of one and the same Spirit, and he gives them to each one, just as he determines." There isn't a lot of room for theological bias in that verse.

One of the life-changing, do-it-again fun things we experience in relationship with God is giving away his really cool gifts to people. It surprises them.

I have a friend who is a prostitute. I met her when I was working in Vegas. We are in different lines of work. I had been talking to her, both of us killing time, when she mentioned her back hurt. I said "I can take care of that. Close your eyes. I'm going to put my hand on your back." Then I prayed silently. After a brief moment, I asked her, "How does it feel?" You should have seen her eyes. She said, "How did you do that?" I said, "It wasn't me. God loves you."

Prayer is amazing. Not the act in and of itself. Prayer is not a magical incantation. As we will see in a later chapter, effective prayer is not dependent on the words or the worth of the one praying. But prayer that partners with God, the prayer that gives voice to what he wants to do in the life of another, that prayer is unstoppable.

God gives through us by praying with us. Think about it: I'm a preacher. As a preacher, I can be locked away and isolated and no one will hear my voice. But I am also a prayer. And what can man do to me! You and I can change the world by prayer, and no one but God will ever know it was us. Sounds like his plan.

Give Me More

God not only wants to give spiritual gifts through us, he also wants to give material gifts through us. That's why Paul wrote the

Joseph

Corinthians and said to them "So we urged Titus to bring also to completion this *act of grace on your part.* But just as you excel in everything—in faith, in speech, in knowledge, in complete earnestness and in your love for us—see that you also excel in this *grace of giving.*

Philip Yancy brought a great story to our attention first printed in the Boston Globe, 1990. A woman and her fiancé went to the Hyatt Hotel to make arrangements for the meal at the wedding. The bill amounted to thirteen thousand dollars, and they paid half as a down payment.

Not long before the wedding, the groom backed out. When the woman went to the Hyatt to cancel the banquet, she was informed that she couldn't receive a full refund, and that she either had to forfeit the rest of the down payment or proceed with the banquet.

It seemed crazy, but the more the jilted bride thought about it, the more she like the idea of going ahead with the party——not a wedding banquet, mind you, but a big blowout. Ten years before, this same woman had been living in a homeless shelter. She had got back on her feet, found a good job, and set aside a sizable nest egg. Now she has the wild notion of using her savings to treat the down-and-outs of Boston to a night on the town.

And so it was that in June of 1990 the Hyatt Hotel in downtown Boston hosted a party such as it had never seen before. The hostess changed the menu to boneless chicken—"in honor of the groom," she said—and sent invitations to rescue missions and homeless shelters. That warm summer night, people who were used to peeling half-gnawed pizza off the cardboard dined instead on chicken cordon bleu. Hyatt waiters in tuxedos served *hors d'oeuvres* to seniors citizens propped up by crutches and aluminum walkers. Bag ladies, vagrants, and addicts took one night off from the hard life on the sidewalks outside and instead sipped champagne, ate chocolate wedding cake, and danced to big-band melodies late into the night.

I love it.

A friend of mine recently had a heart attack. As he was recovering, he felt led to send checks to people that came to mind. I wasn't one of them. The amounts weren't large, many $500.00 to a $1000.00. Admittedly, he whittled his own account down to a minimum, but he's been around long enough to know the difference between a good idea and God's idea. This was God's idea. He sent a check to a young man with a note that simply read "I'm for you."

He received a phone call a couple of days later. The young man said, "I was blown away. You have no idea. I had really grown discouraged. Reading your note and receiving that check meant the world. But I'll tell you what really meant the most to me. I learned—here's a guy laid up in the hospital, recovering from a heart attack, and he's thinking about others."

Recently I was in a nice restaurant in a small town. It was the only nice restaurant in town, a winery set upon a hill overlooking the valley. The dining area is exquisite in décor. The background instruments are soothing, and in this cowboy town someone decided a touch of elegance was called for. It's a nice break from the burgers I usually eat when I stay. On this particular night, I was dining by myself and was served by a woman very professional and precise in her work. She didn't smile often, commented minimally but appropriately, and served me well. At the end of the meal, I tipped her generously. After I left the restaurant, I stood outside to make a phone call. I was surprised when the door burst open and the server appeared. I had begun to walk away, but I turned and she caught me in time to say thank you. A simple gesture of generosity provoked a break in ceremony and a woman to run in gratitude.

The third way God gives through us to others is in our speech. Paul teaches "Let your conversation be always full of

Joseph 29

grace, seasoned with salt, so that you may know how to answer everyone."

Both Greek and Latin writers used the image of salt to picture wit, a right word at the right moment. One poet was praised for "rubbing the city with salt", that is, writing in such a way that certain parties felt the sting of truth while the others were able to laugh. Think late-night talk show monologues.

What's the idea? Conversation full of grace does not mean we talk funny. We don't need to be overly polite ("Why thank you Mrs. Cleaver. What a nice dress you are wearing today Mrs. Cleaver. I like the tattoo, Mrs. Cleaver.) And certainly it doesn't mean we pepper our vocabulary with religious language. I have a friend who laces his conversation with every profanity in the book, and then he ends every phone call with "God bless you."

The idea is that we get to speak what God would say in that moment to that person.

Words are immeasurable in power and worth. They can change the trajectory of a person's life. They can surface deep wounds and heal. They can reach into the fatigue of a soul and lift a person to record heights.

How has God longed to speak to our friends a word they need to hear, and how can they hear when they don't recognize his voice?

I would regularly pray for my staff, and often I would jot a note on a card to tell them how I had prayed for them. One day I walked by an associate's office and saw my cards stacked together. I said, "Hey, those are my cards to you." She said, "I keep each one."

People awake each morning to a cacophony of words. Like a Dr. Seuss book "words, words, words, words." People speak up, talk down, listen in, and shout out. But at the end of the day, when quiet finally envelops, our friends hunger for a Word.

God does still speak, and his voice sounds an awful lot like yours.

Amazing Grace

We don't want the system, we want God. And our friends want us. The radical forgiveness they meet in us, the stunning generosity they can't quite get their hands around—they sense it points to something they're hesitant to approach but now can't help but to take a look.

We are made beautiful as we experience God and give him away. It is never too early and it is never too late to receive the forgiveness that is ours in him. He has gifts reserved for us, ours for the taking because what we really want is him.

And we are surrounded by friends who deep down want the same. The power of grace is in its experience.

In *A Second Chicken Soup for the Woman's Soul,* Jean Jeffrey Gietzen tells about her father, the dancer. From before she was three years old, her father would come home from work, sweep her into her arms and dance. He would sing, "Roll out the barrel, we'll have a barrel of fun," and she would sing back, "Let's get those blues on the run."

They danced until her fifteenth year. Then, one evening, when Jean was swimming in adolescent emotions, her father put his hand on her shoulder and said, "C'mon, let's get those blues on the run." She screamed at him and told him she was sick and tired of dancing with him. She saw the horror on his face and ran to her room in tears.

They did not dance together after that night. After she had children, her dad taught her daughters how to dance, counting out the steps, and she longed to hear those words for herself. But she knew he awaited an apology, and the right words never seemed to come.

At her parents' fiftieth anniversary party, the band began to play after dinner. She writes,

Joseph **31**

My father danced with his granddaughters, and then the band began to play the "Beer Barrel Polka."

"Roll out the barrel," I heard my father sing. Then I knew it was time. I knew the words I must say to my father before he would dance with me once more. I wound my way through a few couples and tapped my daughter on the shoulder.

"Excuse me," I said, almost choking on my words, "but I believe this is my dance."

My father stood rooted to the spot. Our eyes met and traveled back to that night when I was fifteen. In a trembling voice, I sang, "Let's get those blues on the run."

My father bowed and said, "Oh, yes. I've been waiting for you."

Then he started to laugh, and we moved into each other's arms, pausing for a moment so we could catch once more the rhythm of the dance.

Our friends have a Father. He is waiting. By his grace, experienced through us, they will step into his arms and catch once more the rhythm of the dance.

But Not To Myself Alone

One of my favorite coffee mugs, and I am a coffee mug guy, has my name on one side and my standard order on the other: Tall non-fat, no whip, mocha. It's not the shape of the mug or the colors used in the lettering that endears me to it. I hold onto it because it was made for me by some employees at the local Starbucks I frequent.

I didn't simply go there a lot for coffee. I went because I make it a goal to visit the same restaurant, store or bank often so that I can know employees by name and engage in conversation as I can. I cultivate friendliness in hopes that friendship will emerge.

A local video store of mine hired a new store director. One day, I noticed she had been crying on the phone. I left the store, but felt compelled to return. I approached her and said simply, "I help people. Let me know what I can do for you." She thanked me and assured me she would be fine.

A few months later she was considering a vocational move, and as part of her training with a new company she needed to "practice selling" with her supervisor. She asked me if I would be willing to participate. Hesitant, I knew this was an opportunity to give, and I agreed. In the course of the practice session, my background in ministry surfaced.

Though the job never materialized, she remained at the video store and asked me one day what that ministry stuff was all about. We met at the Starbucks where everybody knew my name, and as

I sipped from my personalized mug I shared my background as a lover of Jesus, a pastor and life coach, and explained that I was currently involved in work and lifestyle ministry. At the end of the meeting, she scheduled a time for a coaching session.

One day I received an excited phone call from her. She explained that she had been walking around a bookstore, picking up and setting down repeatedly a book called The Purpose Driven Life. She left the store without it, and decided to get her hair done and called her stylist. A time had just opened up, so she drove straight to the shop. As she was seated in the chair, she noticed The Purpose Driven Life book on her stylist's counter. She told her stylist of the irony, and the stylist said, "Sounds like God is trying to get your attention. He will probably bring someone into your life to explain it to you." On the phone to me she said, "I figure that's you."

We met, and she gave her heart to Jesus. I told her, "Now that you know Jesus, you have the opportunity to pastor your store. First thing I want you to do is pray for your store and for those that work there, and if God brings certain customers to mind, pray for them too. Oh, and don't worry if you are doing it right—prayer isn't a formula."

So she did. A few months later, I joined in one of her staff meetings. Asked to evaluate working at the store, every employee spoke of looking forward to going to work because of the positive atmosphere to work in and the deep care they experienced.

God calls us to pastor where we are. In this sense, pastor is a verb. We are to be agents of grace in the life of people whether they know Jesus now or not yet. We don't need to announce it. We don't approach our friend and inform them "I am going to pastor you now."

Instead, we do it.

The Beautiful Friend

What is God working in us? Along with grace, he is working friendship. God wants to attract people to him by the beauty of our friendship. Indeed, the coming shape of the church will be wrapped around natural networks of friends. Instead of training small group leaders and inviting strangers to "join a group", church leaders will help people recognize the friends they already have and train them in how to better experience community with those friends.

Friendship is important to Jesus. He said to his disciples, "I know longer call you servants but friends." One of the accusations Jesus accepted and embraced to himself was that he was a "friend of sinners".

I didn't understand that when I was *pastor* of a local church.

I used to live with a belief that the mission came first. I enjoyed people, but I figured I'd have eternity to hang out with them. Today was the day to focus on the mission at hand. As a result, I replaced friends with "teammates, fellow-warriors", that kind of thing. What mattered was that we were "in it" together—whatever that meant. In my world, "it" pretty much meant that if they supported my agenda we were "on the same page" and I could spend time with them. Good for them, huh?

It probably wasn't as bad as I remember, or maybe it was worse than I want to admit. Regardless, God brought me to a place where I recognized that people are the mission.

I remember two events that God used to teach me this lesson. The first was when I was alone one day in my office, cleaning out files. I had bags and bags of paper I was finally discarding. I sat on the floor and looked around, and I thought to myself, "Is this what my years of ministry has amounted to?" I doubt Jesus died to save books and reports.

36　　　　　A Life Worth Becoming

The second event occurred often after church. The service would end, and I'd linger around alone. The Senior Pastor of a large church, and I'd be standing there—all by myself. Meanwhile, groups of people were gathered together talking and planning what they would do together. It wasn't their fault. I was about mission.

Of course, sometimes the opposite occurred. People wanted to be my friend. We'd golf, watch a game, catch a movie. Then I'd resign as Pastor but stay in the area. Funny, the phone stopped ringing. Can anyone explain to me why people "befriend" pastors just because of their title? It's weird.

As I look back on my life, the *sinners* I've led to Christ out of my friendship with them were those I knew when I wasn't in paid ministry. How ironic is that? When I wasn't a pastor, I led people to the Lord. When I was a pastor, I led—meetings.

God is working in us so that we never forget he is about people. Ministry starts with people. Ministry is about people. Ministry is friendship, and friendship is ministry.

Friends are beautiful.

That's What Friends Are For

If to pastor where we are begins with friendship, what does friendship look like? A Biblical study of Proverbs reveals four qualities of friendship: vulnerability, humility, conviction and shared experience.

Vulnerability is both an affirmation and an invitation. I affirm your character by my willingness to open up to you, and in my vulnerability I invite you to exercise the same with me.

Vulnerability in friendship is both supportive and attentive.

Proverbs says "A friend loves at all times" and "there is a friend who sticks closer than a brother."

Joseph

One night a number of players on a college football team were having a Bible study with friends. One of the friends, a young female, had to leave the study early. She walked out of the building and across the parking lot, where her car sat in darkness under the cover of trees. Before she could get into the car, a man emerged and grabbed her.

Fortunately, one of the other students had left the building early too, and upon seeing the stranger ran back into the room and yelled, "Hey, someone is messing with one of our girls." At that the entire team stormed out of the room to the rescue of their friend.

One of our girls. There are moments we want to hear the pounding of footsteps running to come to us, don't we? There are times we want to lead the battle cry to the rescue of a friend, isn't there? Friends stick close together.

I am suspicious when people tell me they love me soon after they meet me. I had a guy do that to me. From the first day we met, he'd tell me he loved me and would do anything for me. After I resigned from a church and was in transition, I ran into a financial need. So I sat in his office, explained my need, and asked him for $500.00. I remember his response clearly. "I'll have to pray about it." Huh. I thought he had prayed about it, which was why he was willing to do anything for me. And no, I didn't hear from him.

Contrast that with my best friend. I call him Tree. We have been buds since Junior High. I don't know what he sees in me. I guess you don't forget the guys you hung out with on those long, dateless nights. Since high school I've only been trouble for him, like enlisting him to help me start a church together.

During that same time frame of financial hardship, I called him and said, "I am really embarrassed. But I need money or I'm in big trouble." He didn't hesitate, and the funds were in my account that day.

I'm one of his guys.

A Life Worth Becoming

Support isn't offered in just in a moment of trouble. We support our friends when we invest in them, when we see their promise and encourage their gifts. Benjamin Disraeli said, "The greatest good you can do for another is not just to share your riches but to reveal to him his own."

Vulnerability is attentive. Proverbs 27:9 says "the pleasantness of one's friend springs from his earnest counsel."

When I was in Bible College a church in Winchester, Missouri asked the school to send out a young preacher for them. It took three hours to drive there. It turned out the church met in the guy's garage. He had been an elder at a church across town and left after a conflict. He took one other family with him. So church was the older man and his wife, and one poor family in a garage furnished with a very large pulpit the elder had built himself. I was excited! Seriously, I was finally going to be able to pastor a church.

I don't preach behind pulpits, though, and this offended him a great deal. "Is that what they are teaching you guys at that school now?" he asked. I explained it was only a personal preference and that I could certainly use the pulpit.

The next Saturday I went door to door witnessing. It was great; at church the next day we had a total of four families. Doubled the size of the church in a weekend—how cool is that.

That week I received a letter. The elder fired me. Thought things were going a bit too fast.

I was crushed. I knelt down by my bed and wept. I drove over to the Bible College and walked past the office of the Vice President, Ron Carter. Ron looked at me and knew something was wrong. I told him I had been fired, and he pointed at me and said to not leave. He walked out of his office a minute later and took me to a nice restaurant. It probably wasn't all that nice, but as a young married student in Bible College any restaurant seemed exquisite.

Over lunch, Ron looked at me and spoke the counsel that changed my life: "Never forget, God doesn't want your ministry, he wants you."

When we pastor friends we are vulnerable with them. We let them know our needs, and invite them to make their needs known to us. How does that look for you? Who knows the burden of your heart right now? Who are you investing in? A life worth becoming both opens up and invites in.

I had a woman describe a vision she had for a ministry. I believed in it, more than she did, so I said to her "My horizon is larger than yours right now. One day, that will no longer be true." She never forgot those words, and it was a great moment in my office a couple of years later when she informed me that day had come. Friends need our support.

I have some friends who don't know Jesus. They do know me. They know my struggles, my journey of faith and the questions I raise, my convictions and my hope. They know these things because I tell them, and I tell them because they know I am a friend sharing, not a rep selling.

I figured if friends are vulnerable, I should go first.

Humble Pie

The second quality of friendship we discover in Proverbs is humility. The word itself is not named in a verse, but the idea invades several verses. "He who loves a pure heart and whose speech is gracious will have the king for his friend." Humility is the incubator for the pure and gracious.

Apparently, humility wasn't my strong suit in high school. I opened up my end of the school yearbook. Do you remember yearbooks? They hold a lot of pictures of your classmates and of clubs you didn't even know existed. Space is left for people to write nice things to you, things like "have a nice summer" or "I still remember that night by the lake you wild man you" or "Dear Eric, you are the best" even though your name isn't Eric.

I opened mine and read in big, black letters, "Humble yourself before God." The guy went on to explain that he had come to faith in Christ, but no thanks to me because the intensity of my faith had turned him off for so long. Huh. I figured I better learn something about humility

Humility in friendship expresses itself in two ways. First, "He who covers over an offense promotes love, but whoever repeats the matter separates close friends."

In humility I cover over an offense because I know too well my own mistakes that have been covered. Ron Mehl tells a delightful story of this.

He describes an eight-year-old boy who was sitting in class to take a test. He was so nervous he wet his pants. At the same time, the teacher had motioned for him to come to her desk. When he didn't move, she got up and walked towards him. He had no idea what to do to save him self from this embarrassment.

One of his classmates, a girl, was carrying a large fishbowl down the aisle when she tripped and dropped the bowl. Water went everywhere and drenched the boy. He thought, "Thank God! What a wonderful gift! What a wonderful girl!"

> But then it dawned on him that little boys don't even like little girls. He couldn't possibly let the incident pass. He looked at her and said, "What's wrong with you, you clumsy clod? Can't you watch where you're going?!" As the class laughed at the girl, the teacher took the boy (now covered by dignity) to the gym class to get him some dry clothes to wear.
>
> At lunchtime, no one wanted to sit with the girl. Her friends avoided her at recess. In the unforgiving society of elementary school, she was suddenly a plague and pariah.

Joseph   **41**

When the day was over and the boy was on his way home, he walked out the door and saw her. All the kids were leaving, but she was walking by herself, along the fence. He began to reflect on what had happened that day and suddenly—on an impulse—walked over to her.

"You know," he said, "I've been thinking about what happened today. That wasn't an accident, was it? You did that on purpose, didn't you?"

"Yes," she said. "I did it on purpose. I knew what had . . . happened to you. You see, I wet my pants once, too."

Humility maintains perspective. When we cover over an offense, we reveal to that person their value. Who they are is more important than what they did. The cost of their mistake is still not greater than the price of the cross. I choose them.

Humility in friendship also expresses itself by help in time of trouble:

Two are better than one,
because they have a good return for their work:
 If one falls down,
his friend can help him up.
But pity the man who falls
and has no one to help him up!
Also, if two lie down together, they will keep warm.
But how can one keep warm alone?
Though one may be overpowered,
two can defend themselves.
A cord of three strands is not quickly broken.

Have you ever been helped by a person who then seemed to gloat in it? Three years later, they're still saying "Remember that time your truck got stuck in the middle of the night. Yep, I waded through three feet of mud to help pull you out. I'm still a little sore . . ."

Friends help because they recognize they've needed help too. It's not a big deal—except for the person who needed help at the time they needed it!

The life worth becoming believes people well.

Conviction

Another quality of friendship discovered in Proverbs is shared conviction. Friends hold each other to what they believe. "Better is open rebuke than hidden love. Wounds from a friend can be trusted, but an enemy multiplies kisses." Similarly, we are warned "Whoever flatters his neighbor is spreading a net for his feet." In other words, the friend is not the one who always speaks the nicest thing.

As a young pastor I started a church in a growing suburb. We started well and began to pray about a permanent facility. Without getting into detail, we discerned in prayer that the Lord was going to give us an existing church facility. Soon after, the church did contact us, and invited us to interview to receive their facility. After that process, we were indeed selected.

Could I leave well enough alone? In between being chosen to receive the facility and actually closing the deal, I heard rumblings of indecision. In my attempt to manage the situation, I betrayed the confidence of one of my mentors who was involved in helping the transition. He discovered the betrayal when we were in a meeting and a couple repeated the information I had given them. My friend, Lucky, asked "How do you know this?" They told him.

When he and I got to his car, he looked at me, pointed his finger at me, and said "That was stupid."

And he was right. I got home, went to the back porch, leaned against the house, and slid to the ground in repentance. I spent that weekend seeking the Lord and searching within, only to have him show me my pattern of lying and manipulation.

I smile now when I tell that story, because Lucky and I are friends. He knew I was acting contrary to my convictions, he knew an open rebuke was better than hidden love, and he knew wounds from a friend can be trusted.

Proverbs 27:17 adds "As iron sharpens iron, so one man sharpens another." Friends sharpen one another when they speak honestly, but shared conviction is more than blunt speech. It's easy to lay down the law and walk away, or spout an opinion without concern. Friends walk with friends through the fire of forgiveness.

Forgiving Right

The practice of forgiveness is often sloppy. In contrast, the Bible is very precise in how forgiveness is expressed.

The objective of forgiveness is restoration. Paul instructs us "Brothers, if someone is caught in a sin, you who are spiritual should restore him gently." The word restore speaks of returning to an original condition, and was used in reference to mending a net or setting a bone.

There is an attitude and an action that friends possess when seeking to restore another. Compassion is the attitude. That is why Galatians says to restore him gently. Confrontation is the action. Jesus says "If your brother sins against you, go and show him his fault, just between the two of you. If he listens to you, you have won your brother over."

Paul demonstrated this for us in Galatians 2:

> When Peter came to Antioch, I opposed him to his face, because he was clearly in the wrong. Before certain men came from James, he used to eat with the Gentiles. But when they arrived, he

A Life Worth Becoming

began to draw back and separate himself from the Gentiles because he was afraid of those who belonged to the circumcision group. The other Jews joined him in his hypocrisy, so that by their hypocrisy even Barnabas was led astray. When I saw that they were not acting in line with the truth of the gospel, I said to Peter in front of them all, "You are a Jew, yet you live like a Gentile and not like a Jew. How is it, then, that you force Gentiles to follow Jewish customs?"

Okay, Paul missed the part about "just between the two of you", but nonetheless, especially given the degree to which others were led astray, Paul stepped up and contended for the conviction they once all shared.

Confession is a person's response to compassionate confrontation.

Confession is more than saying "I'm sorry". To confess means to *say the same thing as*. It is to say the same thing God says about it—"I did this, and it was wrong". It is also to say the same thing as the person offended says about it—"I understand the hurt you've experienced". Confession can be very painful.

In response to confession, the person forgiving contributes to the other person's restoration. That's the context of the verse "Carry each other's burdens." Forgiveness doesn't end with the words "Don't worry about it." Forgiveness releases a person from debt, and then seeks to enrich their life. It believes people well.

Someone once wrote:

Forgiveness is like the violet
Sending forth its pure fragrance
On the heel of the boot
Of the one who crushed it.

When I was in Bible College I participated in a concentrated week of evangelism prior to an Easter weekend. I was a freshman leading the outreach team, and we had to drive from Missouri to Ohio. We had driven all night through rain and tornado warnings, and by morning we were behind schedule. I'm a be-on-time freak, and I despised the fact that people hosting us would be waiting for us. Telling myself that I could talk my way out of any speeding ticket, I pressed on the pedal.

The officer who pulled me over was immune to my charm and fined me $75.00 that had to be paid right then in the nearest city. Oh yeah, the name of the city was Defiance, Ohio. God has a sense of humor.

I was mortified at my sin. We arrived at the church, and that night we met with members of the congregation for prayer. In my small group, I confessed my sin and broke down in tears, horrified that my action might affect our outreach efforts (you can tell I grew up in a pretty conservative church environment). They graciously forgave me. The rest of the story is even better.

On Easter morning, I preached and used the incident as an illustration. After the service, a man approached me and said, "I've gotten away with speeding more than I should have. Here is the money for your fine."

He believed me well.

Along The Way

The fourth quality of friendship is shared experiences. "A man of many companions may come to ruin, but there is a friend who sticks closer than a brother."

Nestled into that verse is the image of a friend who has been through it all with you. Shared experiences color the canvas of friendship.

I have a friend who is a doctor. His name is Dave. In high school, he and I were custodians together at our church. Along with

46   A Life Worth Becoming

our boss, we had a tendency to be practical jokers. For instance, one time our church had a nationally known preacher come to speak. Our pastor at the time preached from this huge pulpit that had a clock in it so he was always aware of the time. My friend thought it would be funny to set the alarm on the clock to go off in the middle of the guest's speaking. It did. Our pastor was so mad I think he might still hunt my friend down and revenge the day.

We had a rule that we didn't pull practical jokes on each other. One day something evil possessed Dave and he pulled a stunt on our boss. Bad move. In response, we stole over to Dave's house one night. With permission from his parents, we kidnapped his bed. We left a note explaining that he would have to retrieve it from the church. There, Dave discovered that his bed had been disbursed piece by piece over two acres worth of building, and he had to follow the clues to find the hidden pieces. That was fun.

It is good to know and be known. When my friends and I go out to a restaurant, they all sit back and watch when it's my turn to order. They know I can't order anything straight off of the menu. I want stuff left off and extras on the side. I appreciate their patience.

The greatest ministry we offer to another is to know them and to be known by them.

My college roommate, Bryan, and I had visited a friend out of town. We stayed at his house, and since they only had one guest-bed Bryan and I had to share it. We each got in, stayed to our respective edges, and fell asleep.

Driving back to school the next day, Bryan asked me "Were you dreaming last night?"

I suffered a horrible, sinking feeling. Memory was returning to me. I asked "Why?"

"I figured you must have been dreaming about your girl-friend" he responded, "because I was dreaming about mine."

"I was kissing her", he told me, "When I realized she didn't have a mustache."

Joseph

He woke up to find me on top of him.

That is definitely sticking closer than a brother.

And I really have no more to say about that.

Friendship.

Jesus is for it. He works it within us. He will define his church by it.

The life worth becoming becomes a friend.

That New Might Come

Dale Galloway tells the story of Arthur Berry, a renowned jewelry thief in the early 1900s. Arthur wasn't just your ordinary thief. He was very selective. He stole only from the very rich, and only the finest of jewels. As a result, it became a sign of prestige in social circles to have been robbed by Arthur Berry. As with most thieves, though, Arthur was eventually caught.

When Arthur got out of prison he moved to a small town in New England. No one knew he was the famous jewel thief. He worked hard, made friends and settled in. After awhile, a visitor to the town recognized him. Reporters from all over came to capture his story. One young man asked, "Mr. Berry, do you remember who it was that you stole the most from?" Arthur looked the young man in the eye and said, "The person that I stole the most from was Arthur Berry. I could have made a contribution to society. I could have been a stockbroker. I could have been a teacher. I could have been a successful business man. I could have done all of these, but instead I spent two-thirds of my adult life in prison. I have spent a lifetime robbing myself."

We are numbered among those who refuse to rob themselves. Because we are Christ's workmanship, we know that to rob ourselves is to deny to others what God would do through us, and it is to deny Jesus the worship due him through the glory he expresses in our life.

We understand that we are unique. You are one of billions, but no one else has God's plan for your life. You are a separate canvas upon which Christ's art is displayed.

50 A Life Worth Becoming

Philip Brooks wrote, "Sad is that day for any man when he becomes absolutely satisfied with the life that he is living, the thoughts he is thinking and the deeds he is doing; until there ceases to be forever beating at the door of his soul a desire to do something larger which he seeks and knows he was meant and intended to do."

We are not easily satisfied. We agree with Norman Cousins when he said "Death is not the greatest loss in life. The greatest loss is what dies inside us while we live." We refuse to be like the person whose tombstone read Died: Age 30. Buried: Age 60. We believe better of God, of his grace, of his relentless pursuit of the promise of our life.

We have become convinced that God believes in us. We know it's true because what we have going with God isn't about us in the first place. It's about him, and the faithfulness of his word, the power of his Spirit, and the hope of his claims.

If he said it, he will do it. If he planned it, we can count it. If he spoke it, we await only his timing. God, who is perfect, powerful, purposed and clear, is faithful, willing, passionate and near.

We do not rob ourselves, we press into ourselves. Not because it is about self-fulfillment but about Spirit-fullness. We want all God has. And in God's economy, we discover his best for us in service to others.

Innovation

The third mark of beauty is innovation. Innovation is where the promise of our life is met with opportunity. It is where we do whatever it takes regardless of the cost because for such a time as this we are suited to meet the call. Innovation is the playground for God's creative work through us.

And the future church is innovative!

Innovation falls short if it is only defined as the doing of something new or different. We've seen people and churches attempt the new, and the best that described it was different. Genuine innovation has God's initiative at its heart and results in transformation.

If one of our friends presents a need, and we meet that need so that the trajectory of their life has changed, that is innovation. We were faithful to allow a creative God to act, and his action brought transformation.

If we sound a message, and that message works its way into the fabric of a group's culture so that it proves revolutionary, the message is innovative.

For grace to be fully experienced, it must be expressed in friendship. And friendship is the birthplace of innovation. Man's point of need is God's place of courtship, and there is no need beyond the reach of his creative touch. We are innovative when we partner with God to meet that need, when the promise of our life is met with opportunity. After all, he authored the promise, and he scripted the opportunity.

Don't we love innovative people? And don't we long for an innovative church? We are tired of the predictable. We are weary from the energy of attempting something new only to change course again before it has had time to become old.

If we are tired of it, maybe Jesus is tired of it too.

Understanding The Time

In Mark 2, Jesus demonstrates two dynamics of innovation.

> Now John's disciples and the Pharisees were fasting. Some people came and asked Jesus,"How is it that John's disciples and

the disciples of the Pharisees are fasting, but yours are not?" Jesus answered, "How can the guests of the bridegroom fast while he is with them? They cannot, so long as they have him with them. But the time will come when the bridegroom will be taken from them, and on that day they will fast."

To understand Jesus' response and to fully grasp the depth of innovation, it is helpful to review a little of what we know about the Pharisees.

The term "Pharisee" is most likely derived from the Hebrew word meaning "to separate." The Pharisees formed a society known as a chaber. In order to enter the chaber, two vows were required: To observe strictly the Levitical laws of purity, and to pay careful attention to all religious dues. Each community was organized under a scribe, who led studies of the Torah.

The Pharisees were popular among the masses, primarily because they were middle-class merchants or tradesman, antagonistic towards aristocratic dominance (such as the Sadducees).

Pharisees differed from other sects because of their approach to oral law and doctrine. Drawing from analogy and inference, new legislation was produced apart from the Torah. The Pharisees accepted these as equally inspired and authoritative as the Torah, and taught that such oral tradition had been maintained since Moses. Jesus' conflict with the Pharisees often involved this oral tradition.

In Mark 2, the Pharisees take issue with Jesus not fasting. Jesus responds "How can guests of the bridegroom fast while he is with them." In that day, the wedding festivity involved more than the wedding day itself. Leading up to, during and after the wedding, there was only to be joy and feasting in celebration of the upcoming marriage. Fasting during the wedding week was forbidden.

Joseph

In responding as he did, Jesus makes reference to the Old Testament images of God as the groom and his people the bride, and definitively declares that in his person the groom has come.

It gets better. Jesus also says, "The time will come when the bridegroom is taken from them, *and on that day,* they will fast." The Law only required one day a year for fasting, and that was the Day of Atonement. The Pharisees, on the other hand, fasted at least twice a week according to their oral tradition, and expected others to do the same.

The Day of Atonement is when the sacrificial lamb would be slaughtered on behalf of the sins of the people, a day that looked to the final sacrifice in which Christ would offer himself once and for all for our sins. When Jesus says "on that day" he refers to his death. Then they will fast, for that will be the true Day of Atonement.

The Pharisees failed to understand the time. The bridegroom had come. The one day to fast was soon approaching, the final and ultimate day of salvation. It wasn't time to hold to man-made religion. It was time to party, to celebrate the coming wedding, the day the groom would utter the words "I do".

For a few hours after, the followers of Jesus would fast. After all, Jesus was taken from them. He was buried and sealed. But then the bridegroom returned. Raised physically, ascended, and remaining in the person of his Spirit. The party was back on, and it continues to this day.

When a person fails to understand the time, they are blind to the move of God. So what time is it?

It is time to see yourself as God sees you. You are his agent in the life of your family, friends, and workplace. You are the living word of his message. When people look into your eyes they can see God's heart for them. He has no other plan but you.

It is time to stop feeling second class because your gifts are not on stage, to stop disqualifying yourself because you don't serve in structured ministry, to silence the whispers of doubt because you're not yet ready.

It is time to serve before you've been selected, to give before you've been equipped.

Stage isn't bad. Structure can work. Preparation is helpful, selection is affirming and equipping is essential. And they are all secondary to the Spirit of God in your life.

It is time to quit equating strength with program and to quit centering ministry around the public personality of the pastor.

It is time to stop pulling people away from their relationships and to help people pastor where they are.

It is time to coach, not control, to encourage, not enlist.

It is time to pray before we plan rather than plan before we pray.

It is time to celebrate the stories of people touched rather than the number of hours served.

It is time to quit wasting money on events that achieve nothing.

It is time to risk.

Jesus said, "No one sews a patch of unshrunk cloth on an old garment. If he does, the new piece will pull away from the old, making the tear worse And no one pours new wine into old wineskins. If he does, the wine will burst the skins, and both the wine and the wineskins will be ruined. No, he pours new wine into new wineskins."

Let me offer a simple picture of what this might look like in a church committed to equipping you to pastor where you are, a church that recognizes ministry wrapped around natural networks of relationship.

A number of churches are now involved in "servant evangelism", a strategy made popular through the ministry of Steve Sjogren. I've met with Steve and I like him, and what his church did in their community was awesome.

Joseph

The idea of servant evangelism is to go into the community and serve, no strings attached (a business card telling about church services is attached however). So, churches host free car washes, mow lawns, change oil, etc. It's all good.

Once I met with a church planter. One of his ideas was to do servant evangelism with his leadership team in order to try to reach more people. I suggested this: "Rather than come up with ideas that serve the general community, and then try to convince people why it is God's will for them to serve that day, why don't you ask your core who they know that is in need, and let people team together to meet that need out of the person's love for their friend. Don't tell them it's a church doing it. Just do it. Have Bob call Larry and say, "I know you've been meaning to get those trees out the yard, and I know you haven't been able to work so that you can't do it yourself or afford to pay a service. So, I've got some buddies that want to help me do it. Keep the football game on, because we will need a break and we're bringing pizza."

Makes sense, right. Friends loving friends, no strings or business cards attached. Build relationship. Trust love.

I suggested another application as well: Why do we have small group sign-ups? How many times did I attend the first night of a small group in which I was told once again about how close we would become as we shared the most intimate details of our journey with Christ, only to look around and think "But I don't know half these people?"

Is it possible the church can help people recognize small groups they already have, called friends, and equip them in how to build community with those friends?

One of the observations we make from Jesus' encounters with the Pharisees is that criticism always comes at the outset of the innovative. Why? Why will you be criticized at the beginning before anyone has had an opportunity to see how things turn out?

56   A Life Worth Becoming

There are two reasons. First, the new is perceived as judgment on the old. Sometimes this is accurate (as Jesus above). Often it is not. God is still working to fulfill what he started in what is now considered old. God is still in favor of what is, it's just also time for something new. Like with human beings: He isn't done with old people, but he continues to make a lot of new ones.

The second reason the innovative is criticized is because Satan seeks to derail us. And at times his voice sounds an awful lot like people we know.

For years now the following has been taped to the back of my Bible:

> It is not the critic who counts: not the man who points out how the strong man stumbled or where the doer of deeds could have done them better. The credit belongs to the man who is actually in the arena; whose face is marred by dust and sweat and blood; who strives valiantly; who errs, and comes short again and again, because there is no effort without error and shortcoming; who does actually try to do the deed; who knows the great enthusiasm, the great devotion and spends himself in a worthy cause; who, at the worst, if he fails, at least fails while daring greatly.
>
> Far better it is to dare mighty things, to win glorious triumphs even though checkered by failure, than to rank with those poor spirits who neither enjoy nor suffer much because they live in the gray twilight that knows neither victory nor defeat.

As well, Dietrich Bonhoeffer offered in his *Ethics:* "Who stands fast? Only the man whose final standard is not his reason, his principles, his conscience, his freedom, or his virtue, but who is ready to sacrifice all this when he is called to obedient and responsible action in faith and in exclusive allegiance to God-the responsible man, who tries to make his whole life an answer to the question and call of God. Where are these responsible people?"

They are here, Dietrich. They are reading your words, waking each day to live fully for God. They are discovering in these pages the freedom of expressing God in life-changing friendships, daring to redefine our understanding of true and effective ministry.

But What Really Matters

The second dynamic of innovation is a devotion to what really matters. Jesus understood the time, and so do we. Jesus contended for what really matters, people, and so will we.

When the teachers of the law who were Pharisees saw him eating with the "sinners" and tax collectors, they asked his disciples: "Why does he eat with tax collectors and 'sinners'?" On hearing this, Jesus said to them, "It is not the healthy who need a doctor, but the sick. I have not come to call the righteous, but sinners."

> One Sabbath Jesus was going through the grainfields, and as his disciples walked along, they began to pick some heads of grain. The Pharisees said to him, "Look, why are they doing what is unlawful on the Sabbath?" He answered, "Have you never read what David did when he and his companions were hungry and in need? In the days of Abiathar the high priest, he entered the house of God and ate the consecrated bread, which is lawful only for priests to eat. And he also gave some to his companions."
>
> Then he said to them, "The Sabbath was made for man, not man for the Sabbath. So the Son of Man is Lord even of the Sabbath."

People matter. I'm not going to write "Buildings don't matter. Budgets don't matter. Reputations don't matter." They do—if they serve people. Crowds don't justify status quo.

I remember reading a comment by Frederick Broan Harrris after 300 whales pursuing sardines marooned themselves in a bay.

58   A Life Worth Becoming

He said, "The small fish lured the sea giants to their death. . . . They came to their violent demise by chasing small ends, by prostituting vast powers for insignificant goals."

The innovative never lose sight of what really matters.

I had the privilege of knowing Debbie. Debbie was a young, attractive, vibrant single woman in our church. She taught the 3–5 year old class in Sunday School.

Debbie's company hosted a sales conference in Florida. Gloria Estefan was in concert, Dan Marino, Lou Holtz, Ted Turner and a number of other motivators were in attendance.

Debbie went because she was promised she would be back home by Saturday night so she could teach her class on Sunday. At the event, she pressed her boss for the details of the flight home. Her boss admitted, "I wasn't going to tell you, but you've been chosen employee of the year. We're flying everyone on Sunday to New England where there will be a dinner Monday night in your honor."

Debbie said, "You don't understand. Teaching those kids is the most important thing I do."

He said, "Can't you get a substitute?"

She told him, "I will call and try to get a sub, but if no one is available I have to be there."

He replied, "If they can't find anyone, I will fly you back tonight on my private jet, and we will fly you back here on Sunday so that you can be at the dinner."

We found a substitute, and Debbie went to her dinner. And I will never forget her devotion to what really mattered.

Debbie was extremely innovative.

Whatever you do, please do not discredit the promise of your life, those moments when your gift is met with opportunity. People too readily disqualify their self, too easily compare their self to another and conclude they are less. You have no idea. You have no idea of what God will do with the something that you have. When your gift is met with opportunity, a whole plan of God can unfold.

I don't know her name. But when I get to heaven, I am going to hug my family as they lead me to see Jesus. Then I'm going to hug him for a really long time. After, I will look up at him (he is taller than I) and ask "Where is she?"

She is the Sunday School teacher who led me to Jesus when I was five years old. She was always there. I don't know if she was tired, but I imagine she wanted more breaks than she got. She was devoted though. Despite our restlessness, chatter and impatience, she did what she could to tell us about Jesus. To this day I cannot tell the story without tears. One day when she asked if we wanted Jesus in our heart, I raised my hand and prayed. This dear lady introduced me to my Lord, Lover and Best Friend.

Jesus will lead me to her. I will hug her for a long time too. Then I will look down (she is shorter than I) and I will point to my family. I will look past them and point to the people I told about Jesus and to the churches we started. I will see as well the people I prayed for and any over the years who have heard or read my words, and I will say, "Look what you have done. Thank you. Thank you for being devoted to what really matters. Thank you for loving me when I was five years old, when I was just a promise in small clothes. Thank you for pressing into what God had for you, and for believing when you could not see that your service counted."

First Within Me

Mike Yaconneli retells an account by Barbara Taylor:

> Several years ago a woman was spending her holidays on one of the barrier islands in South Carolina. It happened to be the time of year when the loggerhead turtles (huge, three-hundred-pounds sea turtles) were laying their eggs. One night a very large female dragged herself onto the beach and laid her eggs. Alarmingly, what she found were some tracks heading *the wrong direction.* The turtle apparently lost her bearings and wandered into the hot sand dunes where death was certain. The woman followed the tracks and soon found the turtle covered with hot dry sand. Thinking quickly, she covered the turtle with seaweed, poured cool seawater over her, and ran to notify a park ranger. He arrived in a few minutes in a jeep. Then he drove off, dragging her through the sand so fast her mouth filled with sand and her head bent back as if it would break. At the edge of the ocean, he unhooked her and flipped her right side up. She didn't move. The water began to lap against her body, cleaning off the dry sand. . . . Suddenly she began to move, slowly at first, and then when the water was deep enough, she pushed off into the water and disappeared.

The woman makes this observation:

> Watching her swim slowly away and remembering her nightmare ride through the dunes, I noticed that sometimes it is hard to tell whether you are being killed or being saved by the hands that turn our life upside down.

God is in the change business. His whole focus upon our life is to make us more like his Son. His is a life worth becoming.

62 A Life Worth Becoming

"For this reason, Christ died and returned to life, so that he might be Lord of both the dead and of the living . . . And we, who with unveiled faces all reflect the Lord's glory, are being transformed into his likeness with ever-increasing glory, which comes from the Lord, who is the Spirit"

The Bible also says that for the joy set before him Jesus endured the cross. Certainly that joy refers to Jesus' reunion with the Father. But it also includes more. It includes us. Seeing us, Jesus endured the cross. Naturally, he sees all there is to us. The part we gladly display. The part we hide. He sees not only who we are, but the change he works in us. He sees our transformation.

God is about making us like Christ, in His time, by his choice. I often say "it is a process", but even now I am starting to dislike the word. Yes, it is process, but it's really the natural outcome of our loving, engaging relationship with God.

To keep Christ-likeness a priority is inconvenient, hard work. When I am concerned about another's personal change, I am called to forgive, be understanding, give room and generally suffer the consequences of their immaturity. There are times I hardly enjoy this. Plus, when it comes to my own change, I must exercise patience and hope that others will provide the same so that I can stop hiding my weaknesses and embrace my growth. Sometimes I tire of the process and just want to adopt a good old-fashioned works mentality to feel better about myself for awhile (and a little superior to you).

Keeping Christ-likeness the priority changes our primary concerns. For instance, once I sat on a plane next to a young man who was trying to make a Christian movie. He explained that he was a unique individual, and loved to talk theology when he met other believers. True to his word, and despite my best efforts to hide in my book, he asked me "Do you believe that Jonah was dead in the whale?" I asked in response. "What does the text say?"

Joseph   **63**

Then I said, "Perhaps the more pertinent question for two believers to ask each other from the story of Jonah would be 'Is there an expectation God has of you that you are running from, or are you trying to accomplish something for God in your own strength and understanding?'"

So we talked about both questions. In our quest to support each other in Christ-likeness, which concern seems the more appropriate: That Jonah was dead or that we are true to God's call to us?

But what does becoming like Christ really look like? Jesus answers that for us in his teaching from the beatitudes. The Sermon on the Mount recorded in Matthew 5–7 depicts the heart of righteousness. And at the outset, Jesus portrays the character that such a heart expresses.

When we look at those verses, we see that the last four beatitudes are application of the first four. It looks like this:

- The poor in spirit demonstrate it by being merciful.
- Those who mourn are pure in heart.
- The meek are peacemakers.
- Those who hunger and thirst for righteousness will be persecuted.

But we can see it another way as well. The last four are aspects of Christ-likeness:

He is merciful, pure in heart, a peacemaker and certainly, he was persecuted. The first four are what we cultivate in order to practice the second four, to be more like Christ.

Those who want to become Christ-like are constantly cultivating humility, repentance, submission and strength.

For years I have sought to become more like Jesus. When I was younger, I pursued Christ-likeness through spiritual disciplines. Than I realized the disciplines don't define maturity, they

64 A Life Worth Becoming

facilitate relationship. As I aged, I pursued it in more specialized fields: spiritual warfare, leadership, gifts—I figured the greater my expertise, the sharper my spiritual image. Until I realized that becoming like someone happens more by companionship than copy.

Walking with God and allowing for change through relationship is the catalyst to transformation. And to walk with God, we must constantly embrace the processes of humility, repentance, submission and strength.

Humility

The phrase "poor in spirit" describes an absolute poverty. The Greeks used the word poor here to mean someone who had to cower and cringe like a beggar, as opposed to another word they could have used that describes poor as limited but able to get by. The Hebrews used this word to depict the person who put their whole trust in God. Psalm 34:6 "This poor man called, and the Lord heard him; he saved him out of all his troubles."

Together, the idea of humility is the person who understands that in and of themselves they have nothing—in God they have everything.

One Sunday morning, alone with God, I wrote in my journal:

Into this hour
When thousands bend their knee
I bend my knee as well
With hesitation

Your glory is unquestioned
And my heart is drawn to you
But my life is

Joseph

Still imperfect.

Holy are you,
I am not.

The angels declare your nature
And I am too aware of mine.
Can you look upon me?
For years I was fervent, diligent
Working hard for you.
But in the corner of my heart
A shadow
Whose reach has grown over time
And now darkens
The room of my soul.

I am banking on your grace, God.
I first believed in you,
And then pretended all was well.
Now I will believe,
And press into wellness
Neither shy about my convictions
Nor premature in their embrace.

And so my knee bends
Through the hesitation
To the touch of ground
And there, at the lowest point
I could be,
I meet your love.

Humility is a genuine need that wants what the other willingly gives.

A Life Worth Becoming

Jesus told two stories in Luke 18 to illustrate this.

Then Jesus told his disciples a parable to show them that they should always pray and not give up. He said: "In a certain town there was a judge who neither feared God nor cared about men. And there was a widow in that town who kept coming to him with the plea, 'Grant me justice against my adversary.'"

Here Jesus describes a widow whose only hope for justice depended on an authority greater than her own. In her humility, she persisted. People misunderstand this text and teach that you keep praying until you get what you want. No, the text says Jesus taught it so that we would always pray and not give up, because if we give up we move from a posture of humility to a place of self-centeredness: We either focus on our self as one defeated or we focus on our ability to solve the problem on our own. Jesus taught us to keep praying because to not pray only leaves us to our self.

Elijah became afraid and ran for his life, and God asked him "What are you doing here?" He had taken his eyes off of the Lord and despaired (see I Kings 19). Sarah, tired of being childless, sent Abraham to her maidservant saying "perhaps I can build a family through her." God had promised to build the family but Sarah went after it on her own. (And Mr. Abraham agreed to her terms).

Jesus told a second story:

To some who were confident of their own righteousness and looked down on everybody else, Jesus told this parable: "Two men went up to the temple to pray, one a Pharisee and the other a tax collector. The Pharisee stood up and prayed about himself: 'God, I thank you that I am not like other men—robbers, evildoers, adulterers—or even like this tax collector. I fast twice a week and give a tenth of all I get.' But the tax collector stood at a distance. He would not even look up to heaven, but beat his breast and said, 'God, have mercy on me, a sinner.' I tell you that this man, rather

Joseph

than the other, went home justified before God. For everyone who exalts himself will be humbled, and he who humbles himself will be exalted."

The two stories have in common one truth: Humility wants God. Jesus said of the Pharisees "These people honor me with their lips but their hearts are far from me. They worship me in vain; their teachings are but rules taught by men (Matt. 15:8)." But the woman seeking justice, the tax collector pounding his chest, they just wanted God and what only he could give.

We open the possibility of becoming more like Jesus when what we want is God and what he alone can give us.

One time I was speaking to a woman who had recently become a follower of Christ. She was in the awkward place of knowing that she needed to leave prostitution but was afraid of what she could do otherwise or how she could provide for those who depended on her if she left. When I was with her, she was fighting through a large bout of guilt over her activities the night before. I had my Ipod with me and asked her to listen to a couple of worship songs. They dealt with God's forgiveness and his ability to lift our head. She took it in, and when they were over, said that she felt better.

The next time I saw her she smiled and said, "I'm glad I caught you. I've decided to choose love over money. My friend is coming to pick me up even as we speak. We are going to church, and I'm committed to building relationships there that will help me take this next step." I watched her as she walked away, a smile unmatched in the whole place, a dance in her step.

Humility isn't weak. It doesn't focus on our worst. It isn't afraid of strength. Humility wants God more than anything else, including the convenience of our own way or the confidence in our own ability. We submit convenience and confidence to God and his leading.

68   A Life Worth Becoming

I know very insecure people who are incredibly proud. They interpret their poor self-image to humility, yet because of their fear they hold a tight rein on what they will and won't do for God. They are very much in control, and want God until the time he seeks to push them from their comfort zone. Then the heels dig in. In contrast, I know very secure people, often judged as proud or arrogant, who want God far beyond their convenience, confidence or competence. They seem reckless, but actually they are simply madly in love.

Cultivating Christ-likeness begins with humility, desiring God so much that his way takes priority over ours. We don't abandon who we are or what we can do, we submit them. We belong to God. And we like that we do.

Repentance

Repentance is a gift.

We tend to view repentance more like a visit to the dentist. We know it's good for us but we avoid it. Once in awhile we go in for the occasional check-up to hold off the more serious cavity.

There are two words for repent used in both testaments. One suggests a remorse for sin which may or may not lead to change in life. The other means a change of mind. Biblically, we see repentance motivated by goodness and love for God, sorrow for sin and fear of judgment.

When Jesus said blessed are those who mourn, he used a word that was the strongest of nine possible words for defining mourning. This word speaks of a deep-seated pain, an absolute sorrow.

Once when I was out of town, I walked into my hotel room and saw the message light blinking. My wife had left a voice mail, and when I phoned back she told me my father had died. It was unexpected, and I remember to this day collapsing in uncontrollable, shaking sobs. I had never known loss could be felt so deep.

That's the word Jesus uses. The idea isn't even so much remorse over a particular act, as it is unfathomable sorrow at the distortion sin brings to relationship with God. It is to desire God so badly that it hurts when I am out of place.

So how is repentance a gift? Remember, repentance has both a relational and a transformational aspect to it.

Repentance reframes relationship. Jesus said to religious leaders "I know that you do not have the love of God in your hearts. I have come in my Father's name, and you do not accept me; but if someone else comes in his own name, you will accept him. How can you believe if you accept praise from one another, yet make no effort to obtain the praise that comes from the only God?"

For followers of Christ, repentance orients our heart to the favor of one.

Repentance is also transformational. It is essential to becoming like Christ.

Jesus told Nicodemus "You must be born again." Growth follows birth. That is why Peter writes "Therefore, rid yourselves of all malice and all deceit, hypocrisy, envy and slander of every kind. Like newborn babies, crave pure spiritual milk, so that by it you may grow up in your salvation."

Repentance is not a one time act that leads to new birth, nor an occasional check up for good spiritual health. Repentance is a lifestyle, and the key to repentance is confession. Confession means to say the same thing, and in the context of confessing sin, we are saying the same thing about sin as God is.

Failure to call sin what it is leads to deception.

Jesus said the enemy comes to steal, kill and destroy. Have you ever wondered about the order of that? Shouldn't "kill" come last? I mean, once we're dead, what else matters?

Satan will try to steal what the Lord is working in you, and if he can steal enough along the way he can kill what you were about. And if he kills what you were about, he destroys the efforts of those who were with you and the effect you would have on those who receive you.

How does he steal from us? Deception.

Paul writes that we take a stand against the devil's schemes. The word means "with a road" and English derives the word "method" from it. Elsewhere, the word used for schemes is the word for "mind". Satan's method is to deceive the mind.

The word devil means one who strikes repeatedly. He comes again and again against our thinking.

Satan steals from us by steering us away from the thoughts God has for us.

The New Repentance

Several years ago I knew the Lord was leading me into a season of deep repentance. Dag Hammerskjold, former Secretary General of the United Nations, said "The longest journey is the journey inwards." I had been called to pack my bags.

After resigning from local church ministry, I knew the Lord was asking me to resolve two questions. One: "God, if I didn't do anything for you (like professional ministry), would you still love me?" Two: "Did you really call me into leading the church, or did I just get caught up in the momentum of ministry my teenage years?"

I knew the right answers in my head, but the resolve needed to go deeper.

While in that season, I came to realize the difference between the church's emphasis today on *renewal* and the Biblical emphasis on repentance.

Joseph

In the renewal model, we look at different life arenas and specialize on how to improve issues. For instance, in the spiritual arena, we take issues like sin and Satan, and we seek to *fix our selves* by addressing behavioral change and spiritual warfare.

In the psychological arena, we struggle with issues such as depression and mid-life crisis, and so we sponsor various support groups and resources accordingly.

In the interpersonal arena, we seek to improve our experiences in issues such as communication and marriage counseling.

In circumstantial arenas, we seek to resolve stress, build physique, address loss, etc.

None of this is wrong. It is just secondary.

If we treat the above as primary, failing to incorporate repentance, we enter a vicious cycle of fixing, breaking down and fixing again. Unless change is from the inside out it will never last. Such change begins with clarifying our identity. Behaving flows from being.

Repentance as a lifestyle asks questions about our being. Why am I here? Who am I? What am I to do? How am I to do this? With whom am I to do this?

Right questions expose faulty thinking and confront inaccurate assumptions. They become the compass points that determine our direction, the stars by which we check our bearings.

I have since resolved the questions of God's love and my call. In doing so, I exposed my performance orientation, false notions of God's character, errant convictions of the church and more. Issues I never would have resolved if I was focused only on behavior to correct.

Much of what we characterize as mid-life crisis is a time of repentance. Our jokes work against us. While we laugh at the stereotypical crisis, a man stands at a crossroads in his life. Unaddressed questions begin to surface. Uncharted territory calls to him.

A Life Worth Becoming

It does no good to belittle the moment. Once through this time, long-oppressed strength asserts itself, and more is accomplished in the remaining years than in the previous years. Stifle the moment, and you are left with a painting the artist abandoned mid-stroke, and all you will see is half-finished work and guesses of what could be.

We are afraid of the man. If we allow the outward changes he makes to give way to his inner transformation, our own world will change in the wake of his. So, we joke. We tell him to get over it, to return to his responsibilities, to accept the leash that has been his. He pulls away, not because he no longer loves us, but because we keep jerking his leash back.

Love believes all things. So why do we not believe the man in a crossroads. Did the father not believe the prodigal would return? Did he not look for his steps returning home? We are like the elder brother of the story, judging behavior rather than believing the heart.

The man in mid-life answers:

I will return home
But not the same.
That is not possible.
I return no longer responsible
For another person's choice
To accept me or not,
To draw from me or
To see my strength as a gift.

I return,
Love more pure.
Will you celebrate?
Will you call me your own,

Joseph

Or greet me with contempt,
Placing the blame on me
But carrying the weight of judgment
In your heart.

Does a season define a man?
It cannot define,
But it might determine
If the world is gifted
With the legacy of a life
Or crippled by the loss
Of a man written off.

As I focus on making changes and acting differently, I do so against a backdrop of answers and convictions rather than the expectations and demands of others. Have you ever tried to change because of expectations or demands? If that was the primary motive, it didn't work so well did it? It didn't work because it flowed not from whom you are, or who you want to become, but because of whom others thought you should be.

God has different questions for you at different times. There is no time limit in which the answers must be given. For instance, today, I have new questions like "Do I believe people will love me if they really knew me?" I've been taking my time discovering the answer, but consider what lies at the heart of it. God wants to deliver me from secrecy, pull me into more honest conversations (and confrontations), and free me to be more myself.

What are your questions? What do you need to ask that will reveal how God thinks of you? What are the convictions that need to be in place for change to be lasting?

To become like Christ means that we want him and only what he can give, and that we embrace his thoughts of us. Anything else holds us captive.

In *Will Daylight Come?* Robert Heffler tells the following:

> There was a little boy visiting his grandparents on their farm. And he was given a slingshot to play with out in the woods. He practiced in the woods but he could never hit the target. And getting a little discouraged, he headed back to dinner. As he was walking back he saw Grandma's pet duck. Just out of impulse, he let fly, hit the duck square in the head, and killed it. He was shocked and grieved. In a panic, he hid the dead duck in the wood pile . . . only to see his sister watching. Sally had seen it all, but she said nothing.
>
> After lunch that day grandma said, "Sally, let's wash the dishes." But Sally said, "Grandma, Johnny told me he wanted to help in the kitchen today, didn't you Johnny?" And then she whispered to him, "Remember the duck?"
>
> So Johnny did the dishes . . .
>
> After several day s of Johnny doing both his chores and Sally's, he finally couldn't stand it any longer. He came to Grandma and confessed that he killed the duck. She knelt down, gave him a hug, and said, "Sweetheart, I know. You see, I was standing at the window and I saw the whole thing. But because I love you, I forgave you. But I was just wondering how long you would let Sally make a slave of you."

How long will you let Satan make a slave of you? Confession unwraps the gift of repentance.

Submission

We become like Christ as we desire God and open our selves to his deep work within us. We continue to become like him as he leads us and we submit. Jesus described such submission as being meek.

The word meek is commonly defined as "strength under control." The Hebrew word means "to accept God's guidance as best."

Joseph 75

Together, it is a picture of a person who confidently walks only and where God leads.

The poet captured it this way:

At first, I saw God as my observer,
My judge,
Keeping track of the things I did wrong,
So as I know whether I merited heaven
Or hell when I die.
He was out there sort of like a president.
I recognized His picture when I saw it,
But I really didn't know Him.

But later on
When I met Christ,
It seemed as though life were rather
Like a bike ride,

But it was a tandem bike,
And I noticed that Christ
Was in the back helping me pedal.

I don't know when it was
That He suggested we change places,
But life has not been the same since.

When I had control,
I knew the way.
It was rather boring,
But predictable . . .
It was the shortest distance
Between two points.

But when He took the lead,
He knew delightful long cuts,
Up mountains,
And through rocky places
At breakneck speeds,
It was all I could do to hang on!
Even though it looked like madness,
He said, "Pedal!"

I worried and was anxious
And asked,
"Where are you taking me?"
He laughed and didn't answer,
And I started to learn to trust.

Submission involves two acts: To discern what God wants, and to do what God wants.

Jesus says "I tell you the truth, the Son can do nothing by himself; he can do only what he sees his Father doing, because whatever the Father does the Son also does." Then he says "I tell you the truth, anyone who has faith in me will do what I have been doing. He will do even greater things than these, because I am going to the Father. And I will do whatever you ask in my name, so that the Son may bring glory to the Father. You may ask me for anything in my name, and I will do it."

Jesus did only what he sees his Father doing. That is discernment. Then he announces that "the works that I do, also, shall he do" (literal translation). As Jesus did only what he sees his Father doing, so we do only what we see Jesus doing.

Joseph the husband of Mary rarely gets his merit. On several occasions the angel of the Lord appeared to him in a dream, and the text says "he did what the angel of the Lord had commanded him." That is submission.

Joseph 77

Jesus modeled it as well. "During the days of Jesus' life on earth, he offered up prayers and petitions with loud cries and tears to the one who could save him from death, and he was heard because of his reverent submission."

Submission seeks God's leadership. Whereas repentance is about truth, submission is about trust. Part of trust understands that God leads in his time and in his way. Submission doesn't require that we understand everything. It does require that we understand what is next, and walk into it.

Each year I pray on New Year's Day and ask the Lord for a word that will capture the coming year. For 2006 the word was "unfold." I wrote this in my journal:

Come to me
As never before
Above my misconceptions
Beyond my imaginations
Within my every
Affection.

Come
That I might not be a
Waste
But the finest
Of what you've
Intended

Come
Not that I might be
Acceptable
To some again
But that I might be

A Life Worth Becoming

True
To you.

Unfold
All you've prepared
For me.
Unfold the promises of
Heaven, and
Unfold the realness of my
Heart.

As a veil
Lifted
From the bride's radiant face
As a novel
Stretched
Page by page
As a treasure
Kept
In cloths of care
Unfold.

I found the word unfold to be captivating. It was the image of a careful revealing. If God laid everything out for me all at once, I would mess it up. I'd get anxious, rush the timetable, and look for shortcuts.

Instead, submission simply seeks what is next. And the best way to determine his lead is to follow the need. What situation calls for your gifts and strength?

I had a couple of friends I would hang out with one night a week. Our sole intent was to drive the area, pray, and look for people we could serve. We never put a lot of pressure on ourselves, because we figured God would arrange the opportunities. We have stories.

One night we decided to pull into a restaurant for dessert. Those were the days I could have late night coffee and ice-cream covered brownies and not worry about being able to sleep or stay trim. Those were good days. Anyway, as we parked and got out of the car, a guy asked if we could give him some money. We invited him to join us, and soon he was telling us his story of hoping to return to his home to reconcile with his dad (who lived a couple hours drive away). We offered to drive him, and in the course of the drive was able to share the gospel.

Those were days in which we were just trying to learn to follow his lead.

Strength

In becoming like Christ we adopt a lifestyle that cultivates strength. We err when we think of strength as that which is impressive. If we think that way, then we will disqualify ourselves and yield to the professional and expert. Strength is not what is impressive but what is unforgettable.

The person who is unforgettable is the one who desires God and what he offers, walks confidently in the conviction of their own becoming, is faithful to step into the next opportunity God presents to them, and does so in God's strength and not their own.

I love the story Tony Campolo tells:

> I was asked to be a counselor in a junior high camp. A junior high kid's concept of a good time is picking on people. . . . At this particular camp, there was a little boy who was suffering from cerebral palsy. . . .

As he walked across the camp with his uncoordinated body they would line up and imitate his grotesque movements. I watched him one day as he was asking for directions. Which . . . way is . . . the . . . craft. . . . shop?" he stammered. And the boys mimicked in that same awful stammer, "It's . . . over . . . there . . . Billy." I was irate.

But my furor reached its highest pitch when on Thursday morning it was Billy's cabin's turn to give devotions. . . . I knew that they just wanted to get him up there and to make fun of him. As he dragged his way up to the front, you could hear the giggles rolling over the crowd. It took little Billy almost five minutes to say seven words.

"Jesus . . . loves . . . me . . . and . . . I . . . love . . . Jesus."

When he finished, there was dead silence. I looked over my shoulder and saw junior high boys bawling all over the place. A revival broke out in that camp after Billy's short testimony. . . . We counselors had tried everything to get those kids interested in Jesus. . . . But God chose not to use the superstars. He chose a kid with cerebral palsy to break the spirits of the haughty. He's that kind of God.

Jesus pictured this kind of strength when he said blessed are those who hunger and thirst for righteousness. Righteousness is an active, right relationship with God that expresses itself in right relationship with others. When Jesus says to hunger for it, he uses a word that means "for the whole", as in I want the whole pizza not just a slice.

The strength that develops Christ-likeness is both an inward and outward strength. The Bible speaks frequently of strength of spirit. In Luke 1:80 it reads "the child grew and became strong in spirit", and Paul prayed that God may strengthen you with power through his Spirit in your inner being."

A strong spirit doesn't give up. That's why Paul writes "but we have this treasure in jars of clay to show that this all-surpassing power is from God and not from us. We re hard pressed on every side, but not crushed; perplexed, but not in despair; persecuted, but not abandoned; struck down but not destroyed."

Jesus endured.

For us to endure, we need strength beyond our own. I remember a pastor speaking of his son, Michael, a U.S. biking champion. During one race Michael cramped and couldn't possibly continue the race. Afterwards, Michael said, "All the skill and all the will can't overcome dehydration."

To "try harder" results in cramped spirituality. We are not called to greater effort, but we are called to inner formation.

A strong spirit not only doesn't give up, it doesn't let up either. We are encouraged to "Be on your guard; stand firm in the faith; be men of courage; be strong. Do everything in love."

We can't let our guard down. When Paul writes be strong in the Lord and in his mighty power", he uses a passive voice translated "be made strong." We require his strength not our own because we struggle not against flesh and blood but against spiritual forces of evil in the heavenly realms.

The word struggle refers to wrestling or hand-to-hand combat. It was a bitter, no holds barred conflict.

Jesus never lets up. He secured victory on the cross, and he is continuing in that victory today. He said "I will build my church and the gates of Hades will not be strong against it." He is breaking down the gates. For us to be like him, we invite his strength in us and through us.

How are we made strong? One very simple concept: We do what God wants us to do by letting him do it through us. We pray. We obey and leave results to him. We love against our own inclination. We forgive when we would rather begrudge. We give when we would rather withhold.

Jesus is the life worth becoming. To be a person of grace, friendship and innovation, I become like him. I do so by desiring him so much I am unwilling for sin to deceive me and keep me from his best. I love him so much I trust his leading and I seek his strength.

Jackie was a teenage girl in a small town. She was popular with friends, favored by teachers and active in cheerleading. Between her junior and senior year in high school, Jackie was at a Christian summer camp. There, she confessed to God that she had been living in two worlds, one that sought to please him and one that sought to please her friends. She recommitted herself to relationship with Jesus.

When school resumed, Jackie's old friends invited her to join them to do things they had done before, activities she knew that did not serve her well. She declined. After awhile, the invitations stopped coming. Unfortunately, her friends began to withdraw as well. Jackie's greetings in the hall would be met with indifference. When Jackie would approach their lunch table, no one moved to make room.

Jackie was deeply hurt. But as she prayed about it, she decided that perhaps it was time for her to love the overlooked—the kids who weren't as popular, students she may have been nice to over the years but pretty much ignored.

As she befriended them, they would open up to her. They told her about their problems at home, their struggles in school, and the loneliness that ate at their heart. Jackie would listen, and when it was time to speak she would tell them of Jesus' love for them. And many believed.

As a result, students Jackie had befriended began to walk with a different countenance. They joked around, laughed, and spoke up with confidence.

Jackie's old friends began to take notice. Shortly after the New Year, some of them began to seek Jackie to find out what was going on. Over time, as they poured out their own stories, Jackie would tell them too of Jesus' love.

Joseph **83**

At commencement that year, the town gathered as usual. Speeches were made, songs were played, and names were called to receive their diplomas. The girls would walk across the stage carefully in their high heels. The boys would do what boys do. Then Jackie's name was called. And when her name was called, something happened that had never happened before at that school's commencement and has never happened since. When Jackie's name was called, the entire graduating class stood in ovation.

Then Through Me

Apparently I look like the actor Steve Martin. I've been told this fifteen times now. Ten times people have said I look like the actor Richard Gere. I think it's the gray hair—and the nose.

One day I was standing, talking on the phone in a large, Las Vegas hotel. I noticed a mom and her daughter near me. The mom was holding a camera facing me, and gesturing for the daughter to move to the side and back towards me a bit. The daughter must have given up on that approach, because she waved off her mom, walked over to my side and put her arm around me. I said to the person on the phone, "Hold on, I'm getting my picture taken." I held the phone away from me, put my arm around her and smiled big. The two never said a word to me, but I saw them walking off giggling as they looked at the picture. I have no idea who they thought I was. Steve or Richard I'm sure.

When I was in Bible College I served at a church in Tulsa, Oklahoma. In our church was a professional soccer player named Terry. Terry and I became good friends, and the year I served in the church happened to be the season Tulsa's team won the national championship.

I went to the airport with thousands of others to welcome the team back. Fans were lined up in two rows from the gate to the end of the terminal. I was near the gate. When Terry saw me, he pulled me to him, gave me a hug and told me to walk with him. As I walked down the lane of fans, they were slapping me on the back too and congratulating me for winning the championship.

Sometimes mistaken identity can be pretty fun.

And sometimes not. For years I mistook the Holy Spirit for being other than he is.

The Person and the Presence

Jesus says "And I will ask the Father, and he will give you another Counselor to be with you forever—the Spirit of truth... But the Counselor, the Holy Spirit, whom the Father will send in my name, will teach you things and will remind you of everything I have said to you."

The word counselor translates *one called alongside to help.* When Jesus uses the word another, he uses a word that means *of the same sort* as opposed to a different sort. In other words, what is true of the Son is true of the Spirit.

Scripture describes personal attributes to the Spirit:

- He intercedes, Romans 8:26
- He speaks, Acts 13:2
- He sends, Acts 13:4
- He searches, I Corinthians 2:10
- He can be lied to, Acts 5:3
- He has power, Romans 15:13
- He has love, Romans 15:30

Definitively, the Holy Spirit is God: He is

- Eternal, Hebrews 9:14
- Omniscient (He knows all), I Corinthians 2:10,11
- Omnipresent (He is everywhere), Psalm 139:7
- Omnipotent (He is all powerful), Luke 1:35, Ephesians 3:16
- Called God, Acts 5:3,4; 2 Corinthians 3:17,18
- Named in the Trinity, Genesis 1:1, 26; Romans 15:30

The role of the Holy Spirit is to:

- Convict, John 16:8–11
- Regenerate, Titus 3:5

Joseph

- Indwell, Romans 8:11; I Corinthians 6:19
- Sanctify Romans 15:16; I Peter 1:2
- Encourage, Acts 9:31
- Lead, Romans 8:14
- Empower, Romans 15:13; Ephesians 3:16; I Corinthians 12: 4, 7, 11

When the Greeks used the word full, they used it to describe filling up with an agent that is in full control. The New Testament paints three pictures of the Christians' being full of the Holy Spirit.

At salvation, we are "all baptized by one Spirit and into one body and we were all given the one Spirit to drink." In this sense, we are full of the Spirit in that he indwells us.

Also, we are commanded to "be filled with the Spirit." The structure of the phrase speaks of being continuously filled. Paul contrasts it in the verse with "do not get drunk." The idea is that the Christian keeps in step with the Spirit; that is, we are filled with his character that we might express it in relationship with others. We become as he is that we might do what he does.

Finally, the Bible speaks of being filled in an immediate moment for ministry, "They were all filled with the Holy Spirit and spoke the word of God boldly." These were Christians, already "filled" in two senses of the word, being filled after they prayed. From this perspective, the exercise of a spiritual gift is *for the moment filling*. The Spirit gives what he wants to whom he wants when he wants for whatever reason he wants.

The combination of these pictures is a collage of fullness. The Holy Spirit is God, indwelling us as his own, shaping us and using us as he sees fit.

The Holy Spirit's presence is constant and active. It is why Paul confronts the Galatians: "After beginning with the Spirit, are you now trying to attain your goal by human effort? Does God give

A Life Worth Becoming

you his Spirit and work miracles among you because you observe the law, or because you believe what you heard?"

Paul adds elsewhere that we are to pray in the Spirit on all occasions, and that we worship by the Spirit of God.

Keeping Up

"Since we live by the Spirit, let us keep in step with the Spirit. Some versions read "walk with the Spirit" but the idea is the same. We are with him along the way.

A number of people live under the impression that we come across a need and then seek the Holy Spirit to meet it. But that is more like the Holy Spirit keeping in step with us. The reality is the Holy Spirit is going before us. Like Jesus said, the things I am doing, you will do also—not the things you do will I do also.

Up to this point, we have come to understand that God is making us—individually and as his church—beautiful. The marks of such beauty are grace (desiring God and the things he alone can do for us and through us), friendship (pastor where you are) and innovation (be willing to change and stay devoted to what really matters).

For grace to flow out of our being, we need to become like Jesus Christ. We become like him as we cultivate humility, repentance, submission and strength. Since Christ-likeness results from relationship with God, we interact with the person and presence of the Holy Spirit.

To be made different is not a matter of formula but process, not about discipline in a system but devotion to a person, to God. To make a difference in others is not about our own initiative, strength or ingenuity. It is about the initiative, strength and wisdom of the Holy Spirit.

He knows how to make you. He works his ways through you.

The Spirit has gone before you to prepare your friends for guests, the company of him and you. Life changing ministry personally, and world changing ministry together, is being led by the Holy Spirit of God and we get to join in. Can you feel the freedom? You are not called to figure it out and convince God of your good plan. He's got it figured, and you're invited.

This is the heart of the new day. It is possible for you to pray and be led by God in personal ministry. He is happy to show you whom to love. He is delighted to reveal how to do it in a way that is unique and meaningful to that person. He wants to lead you in ways unplanned. The Spirit is more than willing to design a plan with you.

The life worth becoming is energized by the Holy Spirit. He fills us. He enables us to become like Jesus and to do what Jesus did. The Spirit expresses through us what he works within us. This is the whole strength of our ministry and the beauty of our transformation: Ordinary people giving away extraordinary love making an immeasurable difference, all orchestrated by the Spirit of God.

Your ministry in the life of people doesn't necessarily require training, meetings, budgets and token recognition. It does require prayer, discernment, faith, love and power not your own. I'm good with that. How about you?

So What Am I Afraid Of

I risk misunderstanding in the following comments, so let me be clear at the outset:

- I am absolutely committed to the Bible. By that, I mean that I study to understand its teachings in its context and to apply the truths found there.
- I am committed to Christ's church. I love his bride, of which I am a part.

- Believers who do not embrace the teaching that all of the spiritual gifts we see in the Bible are available for ministry today are my friends. Even if they don't believe in the gifts, I believe they express them and call them by a different name.
- I do believe in the availability of all the gifts we see in the Bible. As I wrote earlier, the Spirit can do what he wants.

I didn't like Charismatic Christians when I was younger. I was raised in a church that believed certain spiritual gifts had ceased, and my favorite radio preachers in high school (yeah, I listened to radio preaching) were of the same theological conviction.

Most of the stories I heard from "Crazymatics" seemed silly (those snake-handling, pew-jumping, chandelier-swinging folk). I wanted my faith carefully founded on the Word, not "experience and emotions". The church I owe my life to was a very fast growing, exciting, evangelistic church, but they taught that the gifts had ceased with the canonization of Scripture. As a result, I was far more concerned with verbal witness than anything else. It was, however, a church that led us to raise hands in worship (very radical back then). Because of that, once I was at Bible College they joked that I was a charismaniac.

Growing up, the closest I ever got to a Charismatic was a girl-friend in high school who spoke in tongues. We didn't last.

I was Class Orator for my graduating class in Bible College. I remember joking at commencement about some day becoming a charismatic. No one thought that was very funny (a common reaction to my jokes).

I don't like the phrases Charismatic Christian or Spirit-filled Christian, because if you belong to Jesus the Spirit and his gifts already indwell you. Therefore, I don't speak of my shift of belief about spiritual gifts as becoming Charismatic—I simply became open.

It happened when I attended a seminar on Healing sponsored by Vineyard Churches. A couple of my friends had gone charismatic goofy on me and I went to set them straight. The first thing the seminar leader had the nerve to do was open the Bible and start teaching. This caught my attention. Slowly, verse by verse, just the way I like, he explained the Biblical basis for praying for healing. And my first thought? "Oh crap." I realized I was going to have to start all over in my study and thinking.

At the conclusion of the teaching time was ministry time or what they called *lab*. I had noticed at the end of the lecture a strange, physical phenomenon I was experiencing. My friend leaned over and told me he was experiencing the same thing. Now I thought, "Weird."

My friend figured that we were supposed to pray for a certain person, and since I certainly believed in prayer I was into it. Turns out the need related to our physical sensations. I prayed and God healed. My thought then was "O Wow!"

I understood at that moment what Jesus meant when he said "My food is to do the will of my Father". It was very satisfying. And exhilarating.

Ever since then, I've just been trying to keep up.

What The Spirit Does

The Holy Spirit shapes Jesus in you. The Holy Spirit serves people through you.

By the Holy Spirit we are strengthened with power in the inner man. In other words, we are becoming more than we naturally are, resulting in different behavior and resilience. We are truer in character and tougher in circumstance.

When you search the New Testament for the how-to of change, you don't find a lot of material outside of simply being in

92   A Life Worth Becoming

relationship with God. There are a number of verses that speak about not doing what we used to do: The stuff that didn't serve us or others well. What we are called to do falls mainly in the category of "whatever you saw Jesus do, do that". And since we can't do that by our own strength, we get his Spirit's strength to accomplish it.

That being the case, our character transformation is in God's hands. He knows what he is doing with you. He knows how to get it done. He is concerned about his timing in you, not the timing of others for you.

Becoming like Christ, by the work of the Spirit, involves both power and process. Power, in that at anytime he can do anything and change you. Process, because at the root of change is truth, and sometimes we need time for understanding and application of truth to work its way into our core. We are transformed by the renewing of our mind.

Tony Campolo tells the delightful story of a man walking when he saw a little girl holding a giant cotton candy. The man said, "That's a lot of cotton candy for a girl your size." She said, "Oh, I'm really much bigger on the inside than I am on the outside."

So are we. The inner strength of the Spirit, however, wants to go outside and play.

Gifts Are Meant To Be Opened

Most people relegate the practice of spiritual gifts to ministries inside the programs of a church. But spiritual gifts are intended to be expressed outside of programs too, in our daily interactions and relationships.

The life worth becoming is naturally supernatural.

Paul prayed to God that "by his power he may fulfill every good purpose of yours and every act prompted by your faith." If you are walking with the Holy Spirit, and you feel prompted to act

Joseph

in a way that is love, isn't it possible the Spirit has gone before you to prepare the way? Is it possible your inclination is the tug of the Spirit? Is it possible your hunch is his whisper?

When my oldest daughter was four years old, she was saying her good night prayers and prayed that her friend's foot would feel better. The foot condition was news to us, so we called our friends and told them her prayer and asked what was wrong with their sons' foot. They said he had just been complaining about it that night but didn't really think much of it. They were amazed and grateful, and promised to have his foot looked at.

I have a friend that doesn't believe in Jesus, and at the time didn't know a lot about my own faith. I was praying for him. I phoned him and said, "I sense you aren't doing well. What can I do for you?" You know what he asked—"How did you know?"

Another time I was in Russia praying for a young woman who had attended one of our evangelism services. As I was praying I sensed that believing in God as Father was troubling because of her personal situation. When I asked through the translator for her to tell me about her father, she told me about a father who was very distant in personality. After clarifying the Bible's picture of God as a father, she received Him as her own.

You have similar stories. Up to now we called them coincidences. There is nothing coincidental about the Holy Spirit resident and alive in you. There is everything creative, spontaneous and ingenious about him wanting to serve people through you in simple and surprising ways.

Believe in yourself as God believes in you. You can hear. You can discern. You can do what he purposed for you to do. And people will never be the same.

Don't mistake the Holy Spirit as I did, as someone who might honor my discipline or shore up my weaknesses. Don't avoid him because he serves as the alibi for the ridiculous and foolish. What is true of the Son is true of the Spirit—he comes alongside and

94   A Life Worth Becoming

changes our direction that we might stay alongside and in step with him. He knows what he is doing, and he knows where he is leading.

The life worth becoming is filled with the Spirit.

In the book *Building A Solid Team,* we read about the Morgret family. They had built a home in Florida on the banks of a 2-acre pond at the headwaters of a creek. 12 year old Michael and his two cousins went to swim just after dinner.

Michael, his head under water, was unaware of the approaching alligator.

The alligator's jaws snapped, slashing a six-inch wound in Michael's scalp and ripping the snorkel mask from his face. The boy began to swim for shore, but the alligator pursued. Michael's mother, Jessie, heard the screaming and ran to the water's edge.

Jessie reached out to grab her son's hand just as the alligator clamped down on the Michael's leg. For a moment, this 100-pound mother was in a vicious tug of war with the 400-pound, eleven-foot alligator. She pulled with all her strength. Somehow, suddenly, the beast let go. Mother dragged son up the bank to safety, and the alligator sank back into the pond.

Michael's scar on his scalp would soon be covered by his hair, and his left leg, broken by the alligator, would mend. The only visible evidence of the attack is small scars on the back of his hand. He wears them as badges of love, trophies of the superhuman force exercised by his mom as she dug her nails into his hand and fought to pull him from the jaws of death.

We live among a people ensnared. Taken by surprise, they have been caught in jaws of death, and they swim frantically to escape. They need someone besides their self to be delivered. So we run to water's edge. We run in step with the Spirit. We grab hold by his power, we pull with his strength.

And together, we rest free.

My Heart As Yours

The things that matter most to me have come from prayer, friends or sex. And since the last two were an answer to the first, I owe everything to prayer.

By prayer, I don't mean an activity. Prayer, if defined as the act of a person speaking, accomplishes nothing. If defined as communication with God, hearing from him and giving thought and voice to him, acting in concert with him, then it is powerful beyond imagination.

The hardest I've ever laughed was watching the movie Meet The Parents. Tears streamed down my face and I fell out of my seat. I could hardly catch my breath. In the movie, Ben Stiller meets his prospective in-laws. Nothing goes well. At dinner, his future father-in-law, played by Robert DeNiro, asks him to say meal-time grace.

> His girlfriend interrupts, "Oh, uh, well, Greg's Jewish, Dad. You know that."
>
> Dad replies, "You're telling me Jews don't pray, honey? Unless you have some objection."
>
> Stiller replies, "No, no, no, no, I'd love to. Pam, come on, it's not like I'm a rabbi or something. I said grace at many a dinner table."
>
> Then he prays, "O dear God, thank you. You are such a good God to us, a kind and gentle . . . and accommodating God. And we thank You, O sweet, sweet, sweet Lord of hosts . . . for the . . . smorgasbord . . . you have so aptly lain at our table this day . . . and each day . . . by day. Day by day by day. O dear Lord, three things we pray. To love Thee more dearly, to see Thee more clearly, to follow Thee more nearly . . . day by day . . . by day. Amen. Amen.

95

A Life Worth Becoming

Awkwardness is the sum experience of prayer for too many. When we first start to pray, we feel unsure if we are saying things right. There is this feeling of talking into the air. We wonder if the person next to us would have said it better. No, actually, we are certain they would have said it better. After awhile, we get comfortable with our prayer but uneasy with God's answers, or lack of answers. Usually along this time we meet people who believe they have secrets to prayer, so we try to practice at this graduated level. Somewhere in all of this, we may admit that we read about prayer, teach about prayer and promise our prayer, only to realize we don't pray like we used to.

A person made beautiful prays. The beautiful church prays.

We cannot interact with God and keep in step with his Spirit without prayer.

Prayer is the primary language of my life. You wouldn't necessarily know it to look at me. I'm not a big fan of all-night prayer meetings. The words "Let's pray" don't send shivers of excitement up my spine—more like goose bumps of fear for what someone might do next.

Not that I recommend this for everybody, but I made a deal with God. If I pay attention during the day, he lets me sleep at night. He rarely wakes me up to pray like he apparently does with a lot of other people. He has wakened me, but not often. I probably wasn't paying attention when I should have been. A deal is a deal.

Yet, I can walk into a room and know his thoughts. I can look into your eyes and discern what God would have me know. I talk with God about anything and everything. My best part of a day is an open Bible, a journal, and conversation with God over my tall, non-fat, no-whip mocha. I would rather pray by myself than with someone else. Where two or three are gathered, I'm not.

I do pray with people and for people, and I do pray in groups, but it's not my favorite context. I can also pray for a long time, but

I'd rather not. Watching people pray, I have concluded that we tend to pray according to our personalities. I would rather play than talk or work, and when I talk I prefer it to be over a meal or a drink. I don't like to be on the phone. When I work, I'm intense and I mean business. I want to get it done and I don't mess around. Therefore, when I pray, I prefer to do it relaxed and on a date with God. If he and I have business to do in prayer, we get it done so we can go play together some more.

Now picture your friends that talk a lot, or describe everything in detail, or need to be around people, or salivate over the word group, or are poetic or musical; picture the dry, the serious, the funny, and the casual. Note the precise, the loud, and the shy. See how they pray?

Fortunately, there are no style points in prayer.

The Prayer That Matters

Jesus said, "It is written, my house will be called a house of prayer, but you are making it a den of robbers." He is referencing Isaiah 56:7–8 "these I will bring to my holy mountain and give them joy in my house of prayer. Their burnt offerings and sacrifices will be accepted on my altar; for my house will be called a house of prayer for all nations."

Obviously, the key image is house. The Hebrew word depicts a permanent dwelling place as opposed to the temporary, like a tent. It was a word associated also with sanctuary and rest. Jesus is basically saying, "The place I dwell, the place I take up permanent residence in, is prayer."

Prayer is dwelling with Jesus. It is hanging out with him.

Hebrews 10:22 captures it this way: "Let us draw near to God with a sincere heart in full assurance of faith, having our hearts

98   A Life Worth Becoming

sprinkled to cleanse us from a guilty conscience and having our bodies washed with pure water."

For years I avoided journaling. It was popular, but I thought it was a waste of time. Why write it when I can speak it?

Then, several years ago now, I tired of my own voice. For whatever reason, I sounded stale. I bought a journal, picked up a pen, and have been writing ever since. However, there was a time in that stretch that I realized my voice had grown too silent. God wanted my voice back, and now I am seeking to discern better when to write and when to speak. Room to grow is among the best rooms in the house, isn't it?

In the end, the key to these seasons of prayer isn't the mode of prayer, it is the essence: Being in the same room with Jesus.

In The Seven Seasons of a Man's Life, Patrick Morley writes "The turning point in our lives is when we stop seeking the God we want and start seeking the God who is."

This is prayer. Drawing near, dwelling with.

What Happens In Us

Prayer that matters is an inside job. Jesus said "Yet a time is coming and has now come when the true worshipers will worship the Father in spirit and truth, for they are the kind of worshipers the Father seeks. God is spirit, and his worshipers must worship in spirit and in truth."

The best way to understand Jesus' words is contrast. If not spirit, what? Jesus' emphasis in this verse was not on form but on being, not on the behavior in worship but the basis for worship. God is spirit, and worship (of which prayer is a part) that dwells with him must flow from spirit. Paul wrote "those who are led by the Spirit of God are sons of God. For you did not receive a spirit that makes you a slave again to fear, but you received the Spirit of sonship. And by him we cry "Abba, Father." The Spirit testifies with our spirit that we are God's children."

We pray from the depth of who we are, in union with God. Truth is the basis of worship and prayer. We give voice to what God has already spoken. Praying in spirit and truth transforms us in the exchange. Prayer begins by changing me.

Jane Ann Clark has said "If you are all wrapped up in yourself, you are way overdressed." Prayer undresses us, and clothes us in spirit and truth.

Since the above is true, then prayer is fun! In prayer the very core of who I am is set free. Truth, not circumstance, threat, or expectation defines me. In prayer I am as strong as any. No one can stop me, judge me, silence me or isolate me. Spirit and truth are bullet-proof.

Shake On It

In essence, prayer is hanging out with God in which our spirit finds voice. Because of this, prayer partners with God. Jesus said "My Father is always at his work to this very day, and I, too, am working . . . the son can do only what he sees his Father is doing . . . anyone who has faith in me will do what I have been doing. He will do even greater things than these, because I am going to the Father. And I will do whatever you ask in my name."

Remember, grace is about wanting God and what he alone can give. Grace becomes us as we grow in Jesus Christ, and prayer is the dwelling place in which we are raised. We partner not because God needs us but because we want him; we partner that we might gain his heart for a person or situation. We pray that we might know his heart for us.

A Life Worth Becoming

Since prayer is partnership, it makes sense that Paul teaches "And pray in the Spirit on all occasions with all kinds of prayers and requests." The essence of prayer is this: We are with God, our spirit giving voice with his, partnering together with prayers of all kind.

Just You And God

We see prayer in both individual and group contexts in the New Testament.

Jesus himself withdrew to a lonely place to pray. The idea in this verse isn't that a lonely place is required to pray individually; rather, the priority Jesus models is time with the Father.

Mahatma Ghandi said, "There is more to life than increasing its speed." Love is not rushed. A people made beautiful, becoming more like Christ through interaction with him, are an unhurried people who give priority to the Father.

It's why I always liked the sentiment of the poet:

I wasted an hour one morning beside a mountain stream,
I seized a cloud from the sky above and fashioned myself a
    dream,
In the hush of the early twilight, far from the haunts of men,
I wasted a summer evening, and fashioned my dream again.
Wasted? Perhaps. Folks say so who never have walked with
    God,
When lanes are purple with lilacs or yellow with goldenrod.
But I have found strength for my labors in that one short
    evening hour.
I have found joy and contentment; I have found peace and
    power.
My dreaming has left me a treasure, a hope that is strong
    and true.

From wasted hours I have built my life and found my faith
anew.

Author Unknown

A Heart Like His

Prayer is how we gain God's heart. Consider what people call
the Lord's Prayer:

"'Father,
hallowed be your name,
your kingdom come.
Give us each day our daily bread.
Forgive us our sins,
for we also forgive everyone who sins against us.
And lead us not into temptation.'"

The Lord's Prayer is really the Lord's Portrait. All prayer begins with one's belief about God. Here, Jesus teaches that prayer
must understand that God is great and God is good.

God is great in holiness (hallowed) and authority (kingdom).
He always acts in line with his character, and he has both the right
and might to act.

In his goodness God provides (give, forgive) and protects
(lead us not).

Since prayer is about the heart of God, effective prayer isn't
about the worth or the words of the one praying. Jesus said, "Do
not keep on babbling like the pagans for they think they will be
heard for their many words."

Instead, prayer is about our desire for God (Father) and our
dependence on God. At times this dependence seems very intense.
Psalm 18:6 reads "In my distress I called to the Lord, I cried to my

102   A Life Worth Becoming

God for help." According to Hebrews 5:7, Jesus offered up prayers and petitions with loud cries and tears. Think of it: He who performed miracles without strain prayed with great strain.

At the heart of prayer is our belief about God. That is why Paul wrote, "Do not be anxious about anything, but in everything, by prayer and petition, with thanksgiving, present your requests to God." The word anxious describes a person who is drawn in different directions or distracted. Prayer draws us into God's dwelling, where our distraction is corrected by our spirit giving voice to his truth about us or the situation. Knowing that God is great and good, we seek the provision and protection only he can give.

The Bible uses a number of descriptive words to capture the priority we give prayer: always, constantly, devoted, attention, earnestly and faithful. What you don't see are words used to depict our performance of prayer, such as eloquent, learned, informed, and moving.

You can pray! Don't disqualify yourself on the basis of performance.

Don't be like me: I don't like how I converse with people. I generally use precise words, often not understood but usually eloquent. It's not the best way to have a conversation, but for some reason people think it's a great way to pray. It's not.

As a person who wants to make a difference in the lives of others, you will pray. The single most effective way we pastor others is to pray for them. It starts in prayer, it is sustained in prayer and it is successful by prayer. You can pray!

Hearing God

People use extreme examples to discredit the genuine. It is unfair to argue that God doesn't speak to people by citing the case of someone who was crazy or criminal because "God told them to."

Joseph

103

God speaks. He doesn't contradict himself, so the Bible is the definitive revelation of his will and the standard of our discernment. For instance, God already said through the Bible "do not lie," so he won't tell you today to lie. Honest.

He speaks in the most creative of ways. At times you will pray and a Bible verse will come to mind. Perhaps, instead, a person in the Bible or a story will come to mind, and in its reading or study you find answers to your concern.

God is visual in communication. We see in the Bible that he uses dreams, and I don't see a verse that says he stopped using dreams. In high school I had a friend that I had recently introduced to the Lord. He and I had been flirting with two girls in our school. While on a church choir tour, my friend and I shared a room. The next morning he started to tell me about a dream he had. It sounded just like the one I experienced. I stopped him and asked about details, and he affirmed he saw the same.

Weird, huh?

In the dream, I saw one girl leading my friend away, and the other hiding in shadow watching me. It didn't feel right, and I told my friend God was warning us. I stopped flirting with the girl I liked. My friend didn't, and the result wasn't good.

Another time, I remember watching an episode of Coach on television. I had been wrestling internally about issues of leadership, and I was having a hard time putting my finger on the specific problem. In the episode, the Head Coach was mystified that he was being held accountable for the team's performance because it was his assistant who had erred during the game. The reporters kept telling him, "but you're the Coach." It was a message of taking responsibility as a leader, and being accountable for those you work with. I sat stunned at the clarity that came to me, as if the reporters were speaking to me.

Well, someone was speaking to me.

I mentioned earlier my deal with God so that rarely am I awakened at night to pray. I have had times when the deal was set aside. Once in particular, just before I was to start a ministry assignment in a church, I had a dream where I walked by an old hag of a woman who was sitting in a chair, and as I passed her she reached out with her gnarly, long nailed hands and grabbed my wrist tightly. I screamed out and sat up startled. After my heartbeat slowed, I asked God "What was that?" I heard in response "Witchcraft", and I spent the next several moments praying intensely about the spiritual climate of the area I was moving to and the concentrated attacks I might face (and did).

God is verbal. I encourage people when they pray to pay attention to words and phrases. It is why journaling is a helpful activity. Sometimes in the flow of writing we clear the clutter in our thinking and thoughts surface that have been waiting to make an impression.

When I pray, for myself or for another, I pay attention to pictures that come to mind, words or phrases that repeat themselves, verses and passages of Scripture that emerge, and any thoughts that seem to take center stage.

Is it possible that God wants to talk you through your growth process? Is it possible that God wants to speak to you about your friends, to have you be the listening ear they are not?

Hearing God has been one of the most freeing dynamics in my life. In any given situation, I may or may not have insight from experience, or counsel that is not contradictory, or a clear understanding of the issues I may face. But I do have God, and I can hear his voice. Yes, he speaks from our experience, and through the counsel of others, and in the teaching of experts. He also just speaks for himself.

In Concert

God wants us to pray together. The New Testament shows the early church doing so. Acts 2:42 says they devoted themselves to

Joseph

prayer. The word devoted translates *strong towards*—it describes intensity in their devotion to prayer.

In general, the church today isn't devoted to praying together.

Leonard Ravenhill never minced words and we love him for it. He wrote:

> The Cinderella of the church today is
> The prayer meeting. This handmaid of
> The Lord is unloved and unwooed because
> She is not dripping with the pearls of
> Intellectualism, nor glamorous with the silks
> Of philosophy: neither is she enchanting
> With the satin of psychology. She wears
> The homespuns of sincerity and humility
> And is not afraid to kneel.

Quite a picture! Despite my aversion to praying with people, I do. Why? Not only am I to dwell with God in prayer, but I am to do so in relationship with others. His permanent dwelling place has a large family room.

When we pray together, we pray for each others' ability and encouragement, and we intercede.

Beginning in Acts 4:23, we see a picture of the church praying together after Peter and John had been released by the chief priests. They prayed: "Now, Lord, consider their threats and enable your servants to speak your word with great boldness. Stretch out your hand to heal and perform miraculous signs and wonders through the name of your holy servant Jesus." After they prayed, the place where they were meeting was shaken. And they were all filled with the Holy Spirit and spoke the word of God boldly.

Jesus said "I will build my church and the gates of Hades will not be strong against her." It is strong, aggressive language. As the church, we wage war against darkness and every place it has its hold. We need a power not our own to win. And win we will.

106   A Life Worth Becoming

Bob Logan, an international church ministries consultant, likes to tell the following story:

> In 1881, the Reverend CC McCabe was traveling by train to the Northwest. He was leading a church planting planning session for Methodist churches. At the time, Methodists were starting a church a day, and in some months, two a day. He was reading an article in the paper that reported Robert Ingersoll, the infamous agnostic philosopher, in speaking to a Free Thinkers convention in Chicago, announced "The churches are dying out all over the land. They are stuck with death.
>
> Upon arriving at the next station, McCabe fired off a telegram to Ingersoll who was still at the convention. It read, "Dear Robert, All hail the power of Jesus' name. We're building one Methodist church for every day in the year and propose to make it two." CC McCabe.
>
> Word of the telegram leaked, and a folk song developed among those pioneering new churches.
>
> The infidels, a motley band, in council met and said
> The churches are dying across the land and soon will be all dead
> When suddenly, a message came and caught them with dismay
> All hail the power of Jesus' name, we're building two a day.
> We're building two a day, dear Bob, we're building two a day.
> All hail the power of Jesus' name, we're building two a day.
> Years later, Robert Ingersoll III, grandson to the philosopher, was distraught and met a pastor. In the course of their friendship, Ingersoll asked the pastor "Help me know the way." Not long after, two infants were dedicated to Jesus Christ: the Methodist pastor's son, and Robert Ingersoll IV

The church also prays together for mutual encouragement and strengthening:

> Speak to one another with psalms, hymns and spiritual songs. Sing and make music in your heart to the Lord, always giv-

Joseph

ing thanks to God the Father for everything, in the name of our Lord Jesus Christ.

Let the word of Christ dwell in you richly as you teach and admonish one another with all wisdom, and as you sing psalms, hymns and spiritual songs with gratitude in your hearts to God. And whatever you do, whether in word or deed, do it all in the name of the Lord Jesus, giving thanks to God the Father through him.

But everyone who prophesies speaks to men for their strengthening, encouragement and comfort.

As much as I like to hear God on my own, I don't see him. And I think there are times he wants me to hear something that is accompanied by a look or a touch. When you pray for me, your eyes are his eyes, your touch is his touch. He doesn't mind the tone your voice gives to his words.

The church also intercedes on behalf of others. Paul taught:

"First of all, that requests, prayers, intercession and thanksgiving be made for everyone— for kings and all those in authority, that we may live peaceful and quiet lives in all godliness and holiness. This is good, and pleases God our Savior, who wants all men to be saved and to come to a knowledge of the truth. For there is one God and one mediator between God and men, the man Christ Jesus, who gave himself as a ransom for all men—the testimony given in its proper time."

In helping start a new church, my friends and I adopted a strategy wherein each of the new church members prayed for three unbelieving friends. The commitment was to only pray, and in prayer ask the Lord to open an opportunity to invite them to the grand opening of our public services.

Our worship leader told us excitedly, "One of the families I've been praying for live next door. Last week I returned an item I had borrowed from their garage. They said, 'We're so glad you stopped

108　　　　　　　A Life Worth Becoming

by. We were going to phone you. We've been thinking we need to get to church. Where do you go again?" They accepted his invitation.

The Bible itself records about a time the church made intercession. Peter had been arrested. The text says "So Peter was kept in prison, but the church was earnestly praying to God for him." The word earnestly means to stretch out the tension. They didn't relax their effort. What happened?

> The night before Herod was to bring him to trial, Peter was sleeping between two soldiers, bound with two chains, and sentries stood guard at the entrance. Suddenly an angel of the Lord appeared and a light shone in the cell. He struck Peter on the side and woke him up. "Quick, get up!" he said, and the chains fell off Peter's wrists.
>
> Then the angel said to him, "Put on your clothes and sandals." And Peter did so. "Wrap your cloak around you and follow me," the angel told him. Peter followed him out of the prison, but he had no idea that what the angel was doing was really happening; he thought he was seeing a vision. They passed the first and second guards and came to the iron gate leading to the city. It opened for them by itself, and they went through it. When they had walked the length of one street, suddenly the angel left him.
>
> Then Peter came to himself and said, "Now I know without a doubt that the Lord sent his angel and rescued me from Herod's clutches and from everything the Jewish people were anticipating."
>
> When this had dawned on him, he went to the house of Mary the mother of John, also called Mark, where many people had gathered and were praying. Peter knocked at the outer entrance, and a servant girl named Rhoda came to answer the door. When she recognized Peter's voice, she was so overjoyed she ran back without opening it and exclaimed, "Peter is at the door!"
>
> "You're out of your mind," they told her. When she kept insisting that it was so, they said, "It must be his angel."
>
> But Peter kept on knocking, and when they opened the door and saw him, they were astonished. Peter motioned with his

Joseph

hand for them to be quiet and described how the Lord had brought him out of prison. "Tell James and the brothers about this," he said, and then he left for another place.

I adore the honesty of Scripture. God miraculously answers prayer and the church doesn't believe it!

In the end, smiles abound. Despite themselves, the church dwelled with God, seeking his provision, and the good and great God answered.

Pray Where You Are

To pastor where we are requires that we pray. We pray because we love God and want his heart for us and for others. There is no program that replaces the power of being led by God to pray for another, doing so, and then seeing God move in concert with our prayer.

This kind of prayer is more heart than art. It opens possibilities that human skill alone could not, and it paves the way for actions that possess a strength not our own.

You can pray. There are a number of things you cannot do. We rely on others to do those things for us and with us. That is why we are a team. But you can pray. And your friends need you to do so.

Once in high school, my friends and I were sitting in a circle, singing songs and sharing thoughts about the week. Our church choir had driven eight or more hours in the California heat, two to a seat, on the bus we had become very familiar with. The coolness of the early evening breeze brought calm and ease to a very hectic day. The park was full of screaming kids and hollering ballplayers—all that a park is suppose to be.

As we met, I noticed a woman watching from across the field. Signaling to a friend to join me, I walked over to invite them to join us. Literally, at the very name of Jesus the woman broke into tears of anguish I had never before seen. Through her tears her voice cried out, "I don't want to go to hell; I don't want to go to hell." For some time I shared with her the gift of eternal life offered by Jesus. Her face spoke louder than words; she wanted that kind of love.

During our conversation, she saw her boyfriend across the park, and she ran over to him. I followed her only to hear her ask him to evaluate his love for her. With honesty he replied in a manner that cut through her heart. He was using her. Again she broke into tears. Now she had fallen to the ground, pounding as hard as she could. Agony. Hurt. Those are the only words that could really describe her emotions.

After she gained a little more control of herself, we talked more. She was afraid to commit her life to Jesus lest her friends drag her down. She was tired of that kind of failure. We talked about the friendship of Jesus, and she admitted His friendship would be more meaningful than those she had now. We continued to talk about her life, her hope, her destiny. When no more could be said, I pressed her for a decision. She had acknowledged the truths of Jesus, her need, her hopelessness. It was her choice.

As we had been talking, her friends came to see what was happening. Now she stood, in this time of decision, between the friends that she had and would drag her down and my invitation to come to Jesus. In a sense, she was suspended between heaven or hell. After hugging me to express her gratitude, she walked off with her friends. How? Why? An indescribable heaviness weighed on my heart as I watched her walk off to a friend's party. No sportsman in the history of athletics ever felt more agony of defeat than was experienced that night. I wasn't alone.

As I had been sharing with her, one of the adult leaders shared with three of four other bystanders . . . they too walked off. Another student tried to share, but he felt a failure because he was in-

Joseph

tellectually shot out of the water. Most of the others were on the bus as people drove by and pounded at its side. Everyone heard the trucks roar by with people cursing aloud.

The war is over but the battles are not. Christ has won the victory on Calvary. I'm good to go. So many, though, are not ready. The enemy seeks them out. We pray because we love Jesus. We pray because we love people. No magic word will save them. No secret will unlock their deliverance. Prayer, sincere, heart-felt, and driven by love, is sufficient.

Your Words As Mine

A few years ago I used to have a couple of phrases that had become a natural part of my vocabulary. Maybe you have some too, phrases like "That's cool" or "Whatever". When something was making me crazy, I used to say "That drives me up the wall" or "That drives me nuts".

One time I was preaching passionately about evangelism and our need to reach people for Jesus. I had raised my voice and was speaking rapidly, and was mourning that our lack of compassion for people "drives me up the wall". Only I didn't say that. I thought I said that, but what I really said was "it drives me up the nuts."

As I was preaching, I noticed my wife stand up, tears streaming down her face as she raced to get out of the room. I also realized rows of shoulders were moving up and down. Of course, in my mind revival had broken out! Surely, people were just trying to hold in their wails of repentance and sorrow for lost people. I preached the last few minutes of the message for all it was worth and ended the service.

Then the laughter broke. You wouldn't believe how many people rushed to the altar, not to repent but to ask me "Do you know what you said?"

I've said worse. Pulpit bloopers can be pretty funny, like my friend who was trying to say that Lot pitched his tents toward Sodom, only to say Lot pinched his tits. I thought he might get fired for that one.

The life worth becoming seeks a heart like God's, which is why we pray. It also seeks for his words to be ours, which is why we spend time with God in the Bible. Getting our own words wrong can be funny, but getting God's word right is critical to our transformation.

Nothing But The Truth

Debate about the nature of Scripture has raged throughout every generation. Respected leaders today, devoted to Christ Jesus, have raised new issues concerning the basis by which we interpret the Bible. I doubt God panics over the discussion, and this book is not intended to join the debate. Suffice it to say that a word or passage means what the author intended it to mean at that time, and that a word or passage is used by God for all time to communicate or accomplish what he wants in a given moment.

Instead, this chapter's focus is on wanting God so much we can't get enough of his word, and loving friends so much we don't deny them the value of his word.

I have referred to a time I was in Murmansk, Russia on an evangelistic mission. It was filled with miracle and memory. But one of the clearest memories is of a friend who leads worship. We were on the plane flying over the Atlantic. Many of the passengers were asleep including most of our team. I woke up and looked around, and there in his seat was my friend with the Bible open on his lap, just spending time with his God.

Too few people want God so much they hunger for his word, seeking it for them selves, and they remain content that their relationship with the Bible is second-hand through the teaching of others.

It takes the word of Christ to shape the work of Christ in you.

It takes the vocabulary of the Spirit to sound the voice of the Spirit.

The first followers of Christ understood this. That is why they "devoted them selves to the apostle's teaching," and why Paul encouraged young Timothy to "devote yourself to the public reading of Scripture, to preaching and to teaching."

You Gotta Love It

Psalm 119 is David's longest psalm and is focused on God's word. He wrote:

- I rejoice in following your statutes as one rejoices in great riches. I meditate on your precepts and consider your ways. I delight in your decrees; I will not neglect your word (vs. 14–16).
- The law from your mouth is more precious to me than thousands of pieces of silver and gold (v. 72).
- Oh, how I love your law! I meditate on it all day long (v. 97).
- How sweet are your words to my taste, sweeter than honey to my mouth (v. 103).

God intended for our relationship with him to be served by his word. God speaks, and he has spoken. Those who want to be like Christ and to influence others for him are those who love his word.

This Book We Call The Bible

No other literature has been as preserved as the Bible. It was written progressively over a period of about 1600 years. Moses had the book of the law preserved in the tabernacle (Deuteronomy 31:24). The king was to write for himself a copy of the law on a scroll (Deuteronomy 17:18). While in captivity, Ezra had the law in his hand. Today, in whole or in part, more than 5000 manuscripts of

116   A Life Worth Becoming

the New Testament in its original language are known, far surpassing the preservation of any other written document.

Why such preservation? Perhaps it is because God considers it to be more than a book.

The Bible was given by inspiration: "All Scripture is inspired by God." Inspiration means that God put the messages in the mind of men. It doesn't mean it was dictated or void of the writer's skill and style.

The Bible claims to be the word of God. Moses said "These are the commands, decrees and laws the Lord your God directed me to teach you to observe in the land that you are crossing the Jordan to possess . . ." Jesus affirmed the Old Testament to be revelation from God when he said "If he called them 'gods' to whom the word of God came—and the Scriptures cannot be broken . . ." And Peter wrote "Above all, you must understand that no prophecy of Scripture came about by the prophet's own interpretation. For prophecy never had its origin in the will of man, but men spoke from God as they were carried along by the Holy Spirit."

Additionally, the New Testament claims revelation for itself. Peter wrote of Paul:

> Bear in mind that our Lord's patience means salvation, just as our dear brother Paul also wrote you with the wisdom that God gave him. He writes the same way in all his letters, speaking in them of these matters. His letters contain some things that are hard to understand which ignorant and unstable people distort, as they do the other Scriptures, to their own destruction.

Don't you love Peter's honesty! "Yeah, Paul's hard to understand some times, but it's Scripture."

Of course, the divine origin of Scripture is not supported by claim alone. The very character of the book supports its claim. For instance, prophecies within it are fulfilled hundreds of years later. People over the years have testified to its effect in their lives. Time and energy have been invested in its translation, copying and distribution.

Why? Perhaps it is because people consider it to be more than a book.

To love the Bible is not to repeat the error of the Pharisees. Jesus admonished "You diligently study the Scriptures because you think that by them you possess eternal life. These are the Scriptures that testify about me, yet you refuse to come to me to have life." No, to love the Bible is to want God so much you seek him on every page, in order that the God of the pages might write his character indelibly on your heart.

And So It Is

Those who want to know Christ and make him known cultivate God's word in their life through two practices.

First, they establish the authority of God's word in their life. The early believers devoted themselves to the apostles teaching. The Bible says of the Bereans that they "were of more noble character than the Thessalonians for they received the message with great eagerness and examined the Scriptures every day to see if what Paul said was true." And Paul wrote "stand firm and hold to the teachings we passed on to you whether by word of mouth or by letter."

Establishing God's word as authority in our life means we are constantly exposing ourselves to Biblical teaching, carefully examining the teaching for truth, and confidently living it out.

As I have confessed, I used to listen to radio preaching. I was addicted to one teacher in particular, rarely missing a broadcast and regularly ordering his tapes and study notes. The positive side

A Life Worth Becoming

of this is that I was being taught. The downside was that I concluded anyone who studied as much as he did must be right in everything they teach. It wasn't until I learned how to study for myself that I corrected that perception.

If I were coaching you right now, I would ask, "How will you put yourself in a place where you are receiving Biblical teaching?" The resources, of course, are tremendous: local church preaching, television, radio, tape and CD, book, print and internet.

And then I would ask, "How will you know the teaching is true?" I remember sitting in a preaching class my senior year at Bible College, and one of the students preaching that day confessed to being nervous because I was seated on the front row with my Bible open checking the accuracy of everything he said (I wasn't always easy to get along with).

Admittedly, well-meaning, Jesus-loving, heaven-destined people disagree. The issue isn't that everyone will agree with your conclusions. The issue is that your conclusions are drawn from your Biblical studies and not the popularity, charisma or reputation of a teacher. One of the most frequently asked questions people hear me say, with a gentle and charming disposition of course, is "I know that's what you have heard, but what does the Bible say? Let's find it together."

For instance, I teach that women are free to exercise any spiritual gift. Gifts are not gender restricted. I learned this from the Bible. Some people disagree—strongly. One such man joined me for a breakfast after I preached a controversial message on women ministering. He tossed copies from a commentary at me and said "I think you should read this." It is hard to offend me but he managed it, even more than the time my seventh grade teacher called me the scum of the earth in front of the whole class. Surprisingly, after years of studies and degrees, I actually had managed to read

Joseph

that commentary before that day. I would have been more impressed if the guy had said "Can we look at these verses together?"

Read the Bible to see if something is so. You are not called to parrot popular teaching. The Bible is not authority for you if it is without personal conviction. To simply believe what another says because you like them or because they seem so studied is to treat teaching as a magic potion.

Okay, So How?

To establish God's Word as authority in our life means that we are concerned about the context, content and conversion of a verse or passage.

The context seeks to understand a verse in its historical and Biblical place.

From a historical perspective, I want to know who wrote the text when, to whom it was written and why. Additionally, I want to know the political and social influences of the time it was written. For instance, much of the discussion of women in ministry is informed by a knowledge of the religious practices of cults in Corinth and Ephesus, the social esteem of women in those societies and the developmental stages of churches in that time.

From a Biblical perspective, I try to understand context by starting from the larger frame to smaller frames of reference. Is the passage in the Old Testament or New Testament? Is it in historical books, poetic books or prophetic books? Is it gospels or letters? What kind of literature is represented in the passages before and after the text (is it preceded by a poem, or Old Testament reference or a song)? Is the author arguing or informing? These questions allow the reader to understand lines of thought and intent.

120   A Life Worth Becoming

For example, Paul's argument for the behavior of women in church in Corinth is written in the context of a corrective letter confronting abuse. His comments about women teaching in I Timothy is in the context of a letter informing his disciple of how church should be conducted given the rise of false teaching and cultic influences in Ephesus. Should those two different contexts be taken into consideration when trying to form an understanding about women in leadership and ministry in a local church?

I once had a disagreement with a fellow pastor about speaking in tongues. He argued his case from the narrative of Acts. I argued mine from the letter of I Corinthians. After all, First Corinthians was written to address needed corrections and therefore clearly spells out Paul's teachings and principles, whereas a narrative simply allows one to understand what was true of a person's experience at the time. In narrative, it *happened.* In instruction, it *should happen.*

Good commentaries that include history are a great way of understanding historical context. Read several to increase your knowledge.

Context clarifies perspective and colors understanding.

The content of a passage is authoritative if we fully observe and rightly interpret what it says. I observe in order to see well; I interpret in order to think well.

In observing a text, I am asking questions to help me determine the facts, feeling and flags of a passage. The *facts* answer questions of who, what, when, where, why and how. The type of literature and mood of a passage gives me a *feel* for where the author is coming from. Are they angry, triumphant, concerned or happy? The *flags* of a passage can be determined by words or phrases that seem key, repeated and visual. "Therefore" is a flag that leads to understanding (*wherefore is the therefore there for* as my profs used to say).

Joseph

In his book *Leap Over a Wall,* Eugene Peterson makes this observation from Psalm 51:

> Psalm 51 does it right: there are only four different words used to name the sin, so it's out in the open where it can be faced. These four sin-words are sufficient to adequately map the entire country of sin. But the central action is carried by nineteen different verbs used to invoke or declare God's action of forgiveness and restoration. We have a finite number of ways to sin; God has an infinite number of ways to forgive.

That's a beautiful observation!

To interpret I concern myself with what a word or phrase means. Vine's Expository Dictionary and other references are helpful to this end. For instance, you saw me make an observation of Jesus' use of poor in Matthew 5. He didn't use a word meaning to just get by, he used a word meaning destitute, calling for complete reliance on God. The distinction is important. The poor in spirit are not those who occasionally call on God when their own efforts failed; the poor in spirit depend every day on God.

After understanding the context and content of a verse or passage, I convert it from a place on a page to a place in my heart: How does God want this to effect me? At this point, I want to know what the text is saying about God and how I should regard him, or about me and how I should affirm or change attitudes and behavior. Conversion takes a current circumstance and understands it against the backdrop of those who experienced the same in the Bible. Converting a text never contradicts its context or content. It takes it from *way back then* to *right here and now.*

Of course, the truth of the Scripture is authority, not my understanding of what it means. We must give ourselves room to clarify our thinking. We are seeking to solidify our understanding of truth, and our search doesn't end with what another says.

A Life Worth Becoming

Why is this so important? The concept of authority in the church today is horribly abused. We are being told to come under the authority of a leader. Scripture is clear: God's word is authority, and only as it is being accurately taught and applied is its authority being exercised. We are all subject to the word of God, teacher and student alike. A Pastor does not hold authority by his position or title: Authority is held in the truth of the word.

Further, when Paul says to stand firm and hold to the teachings we have received, he uses terminology that speaks of prevailing or overcoming. Not everyone agrees with what God says. People we love don't necessarily give the same place to God's word as we do. People who don't love us may especially question our thinking. We are not only strong against such criticism, confident in what we have learned, but we shape ourselves by Biblical truth, overcoming criticism not just by argument but by transformation.

A changed life is pretty good evidence in itself.

We embrace God's word as we establish its authority and as we work out its application in our life. That is why Paul would write:

- "I myself am convinced, my brothers, that you yourselves are full of goodness, complete in knowledge and competent to instruct one another."
- "Let the word of Christ dwell in you richly as you teach and admonish one another with all wisdom."

Authority is found in the text of the apostles' teaching. The application is worked out as we practice its truth and share it with one another. That is the progression Paul refers to: We enjoy goodness as a result of applying God's truth, completing what we have learned and therefore able to instruct others through our understanding, example and testimony.

Because Biblical truth is central to spiritual growth, the Bible warns against false teaching repeatedly, especially in later letters

Joseph

when such teaching was beginning to predominate. Specifically, Paul urged Timothy to "command certain men not to teach false doctrines any longer, nor to devote themselves to myths and endless genealogies. These promote controversies rather than God's work." And "Warn them before God against quarreling about words; it is of no value, and only ruins those who listen . . . Avoid godless chatter, because those who indulge in it will become more and more ungodly."

The primary emphasis is on avoiding controversies, which refers to arguments and disputes. The word chatter is a cousin to the idea, and means empty talk. We are called to truth and its application, not simply thoughts and a new way to dress them.

How are you applying Biblical teaching? What have you discovered about God in Scripture that changes your thinking about him and your relationship with him? What Biblical character do you relate to, and what did they do well that you can emulate or do wrong that you can avoid? What current teachings are popular but you've never studied for yourself to see if it is so?

To pastor where we are, we live by authority that never changes so that we can live by truth that never fails. Our own experience allows us to speak into situations friends find themselves in, in a language they understand but with Biblical insight they may not know.

Tony Campolo tells about Tomas Borge, the Nicaraguan freedom fighter, who lived by such authority and truth.

> During the revolution, Borge was captured and put in a dungeon. There he was chained to the wall, and in his helpless condition, was forced to watch as his captors dragged in his wife and gang raped her in front of him. Then they castrated him in an attempt to take away the last vestiges of his manhood.
>
> When the revolution succeeded, Tomas Borge was released, and he paraded before the cheering crowds of Nicaragua as one of

124   A Life Worth Becoming

the nation's heroes. But as he marched, he noticed in the crowd the face of one of his captors. It was one of the men who had raped his wife.

Borge broke ranks from the parade, ran over to where the man was standing, grabbed him by the shoulders, shook him, and yelled, "Do you remember me? Do you remember me? Do you remember me?"

The trembling man pretended he had never seen Borge before. But Borge persisted and screamed, "I will never forget your face! I will never forget it!" Then he asked, "Now do you know what this revolution is all about? Now do you understand this revolution?"

The trembling and confused man could only answer in his fear, "Yes! Yes!"

Borge responded, "No! You don't understand what this revolution is all about!" Then he embraced the man and shouted, "I forgive you! I forgive you! That's what this revolution is all about!"

It takes the word of Christ to shape the work of Christ in us.

Unleashed. Unstoppable.

Rodney L. Cooper, Ph.D. tells of a young man named Joe who attended a professional truck driving school. At the end of his training, he had to take an oral exam as part of the graduation requirement. The trainer posed certain hypothetical situations, including this one.

"Now, Joe, you've just peaked the top of a mountain with a full load, and you're now descending at about fifty-five miles per hours. You see a gentle curve up ahead, and you know that to take it safely you have to put on the brakes. But, Joe, you discover you don't have any brakes, so you barely make it around the curve. Now you're going sixty-five to seventy miles per hour, and you know you have to slow this rig down, so you reach for the emergency brake and pull with all you have, only to find that you don't have an emergency brake anymore either. You are now going eighty to ninety, and you have to slow this rig down somehow, so you look for an open space you can pull off into. But Joe, you can't do that because you have two ninety-foot gullies on each side of you. And to top it all off, Joe, you are now going a hundred miles per hour, and right at the bottom of the mountain is a freight train stopped and loaded down. Now, Joe, what are you going to do? How are you going to get out of this?"

Joe thought for a minute and then responded, "I'd wake up John who's sleeping in the back."

"Why would you wake up John?" the instructor asked.

"Because he's never seen a wreck like this one before!"

Can you relate?

There are times we all feel penned in with no way out and no where to turn. Circumstances weight us down and critics keep us down. Ingenuity will not serve us, and the degree of thinking that led us in certainly won't lead us out. We can only brace ourselves for the crash.

Too many of us live hoping to survive the inevitable. We wait for the next wave of trouble to pass over us. Grateful we didn't drown, we consider ourselves fortunate. We are consoled that things could be worse. We tell ourselves that we have another day, as if time is the measure of our accomplishment.

But when you live in the light of eternity, time is opportunity, not success. God does not make us new in order to survive and stretch our days. He makes us like his Son that we might overcome. In Christ, we win! We defeat what would hold us back. Circumstances are stripped of power and critics are silenced. We grow in him through trial and despite small people.

Jesus did not survive the cross. He rose above it.

If we are to made more like Jesus, and if in our relationship with him we are to become an unforgettable, positive influence in the lives of others, we do so living in the power and promise of the resurrection. Circumstances do not determine our future. Critics do not define us. What God does in us and through us, and what God says of us is sufficient.

This is faith and freedom.

Faith believes in God. That is propositional. There are teachings and assertions about God that faith embraces as true. It is essential truth we bet our life on.

Faith believes God. That is possibility. For instance, a person has a great need and we believe God will meet that need. We may not be personally involved, but we hope in his character on behalf of another.

Joseph 127

Faith follows God. That is partnership. God initiates and we accept. Personal transformation does not result from a faith alone that is propositional, or even from faith that believes God to do the impossible. Change flows from faith that is in partnership with what God does in us and through us.

Freedom, according to Biblical Greek usage, is the ability to go wherever one wants. The idea is that God has sin fenced in, not man. Culture would have us believe otherwise. It is often portrayed that to follow Christ is to live boxed in, to be unable to do what you want, to watch from behind bars while others willingly play and have fun.

On the contrary, God has sin caged behind barbed wire. In Christ, the opportunities are boundless. It is why certain words for sin, such as trespass, help paint a clear picture. We climb over the fence into sin and find ourselves trapped, watching others live free while we are "prisoners of our own device".

Freedom walks in open terrain. Guided by God's word I am not taken captive by opinion. Led by his Spirit, I am not restrained by tradition or expectation.

Without faith and freedom, the Spirit is at best a friend but not a force; prayer is meaningful but moves nothing; the Bible is wisdom with dust.

The Only Thing That Counts

My favorite verse is Galatians 5:6 "The only thing that counts is faith expressing itself through love." The Greek read word behind "only thing that counts" speaks of intensive strength, the power that accomplishes what it sets out to do. The word "expressing" translates a word we've seen earlier for work, the strain that pushes through. In other words, the only thing that will accomplish what God has for us is faith driven to the extreme by love.

When the Bible pictures this kind of faith, it gives us four images of partnership we are to realize with God. The first image is obedience. Paul wrote "Through him and for his name's sake, we received grace and apostleship to call people from among all the Gentiles to the obedience that comes from faith." The word obedience means to *hear under,* and it is the idea of listening in order to follow.

The second image is turning. "They tell how you turned to God from idols to serve the living and true God." The word turn indicates an *immediate and decisive choice.*

The third image is shared gifts. Paul confessed "I long to see you that I may impart to you some spiritual gift to make you strong—that is, that you and I may be mutually encouraged by each other's faith." The word encouraged is the word we have for *helper,* and is used to describe the Holy Spirit, one called alongside to help. So, we are never more an agent of the Holy Spirit than when we come alongside another to help, expressing the Spirit in us through us.

The fourth image of faith as partnership returns us to the idea of work. Paul told the Thessalonians that he remembered their work produced by faith, literally *work of faith.*

Together, faith is portrayed as listening to God in order to follow, immediately and decisively choosing him and his lead, giving away what he gives to us and pressing through every obstacle so that God's purpose might be realized. It is doing God's will, God's way with people we love. The life worth becoming lives by faith.

The alternative is boring. God's voice is crowded out by careful analysis and majority rule. Cautious calculation delays decision. Merit and resume qualify ministry instead of divine selection. Faith becomes the last resort of failed effort.

I have stories of faith from my youth. But quickly, in the exuberance of growth, I easily came to rely more on skill and sense than faith. God still worked, and people were still helped, but my faith became limited. Yes, I believed in God, and yes, I believed God. Too often, though, I ventured out on my own and invited him along.

Though my faith slumbered, I was jarred awake in the middle of an argument in Bible College. The class and professor were discussing the proposition "It is never right to lie." Students were raising scenarios like this: "If we are smuggling Bibles into a country where they are forbidden, it would be right to lie in order to serve the greater good."

The professor responded with a story about Corrie Ten Boom, and a time when she hid Jews under her dining table when Nazi soldiers came to her door. Upon asking if she were hiding anyone, she told them they were under the table. The soldiers didn't believe her and never looked. I never verified that story, but it didn't matter. What shook me was what my professor said next. "If you can't trust God with the truth, what do you have a God for?"

That question, "What do you have a God for?" has never left me. It alone was worth the tuition.

The old conservative in me wants to defend the phrase. I know right now that someone is thinking "we don't have a God for anything—he's not Santa yielding to our every whim." But I won't defend it. Think in terms of what Paul said in Galatians 3:3 "After beginning with the Spirit, are you now trying to attain your goal by human effort?" That's the point. Do we rely on God or on our own instinct and reason?

Pleasing God

Hebrews 11:6 teaches "Without faith it is impossible to please God." Now it makes sense, doesn't it? He wants us to listen, to respond, to give, to press through. Why? Only then is he truly known by us and in us. He is the Creator. We, by nature, limit his creativity.

130　　　　　A Life Worth Becoming

He, by nature, expands ours. He is a lot more fun than we. All of our best for him is tarnished glory. All of his best through us is transparent glory.

When we pastor where we are, we do so out of faith and in freedom. We partner with God in the lives of people. We look for his initiative and tag along to do our part. We are unleashed and unstoppable.

What does such faith look like? When we review Hebrews 11, we observe eight expressions of faith.

Faith is in *ready* position

This is familiar language for the athlete. Before the pitch, snap or pass of the ball, players are in ready position to respond. Verse 7 says that Noah, "when warned about things not yet seen", built an ark to save his family.

Noah didn't need to understand everything about God's plan, he just needed to understand his own next move. He needed to be ready. The investigative show 60 Minutes once asked Coach Bobby Knight, then the basketball coach of the national champion Indiana Hoosiers, why his basketball teams were always so successful. Knight answered, "The will to succeed is important, but I'll tell you what's more important: It's the will to prepare"

What does readiness mean for you today? God may have given you a vision, but he's also given you a step. What are you to build in yourself in preparation for God's rains? How is he making his voice distinct that you might make your response immediate and decisive? Maybe you are learning to pray so that you can discern God's leading more clearly when he calls you to serve a friend. Perhaps you are studying the Bible to increase its authority and application.

Joseph 131

In 1952, Edmund Hillary attempted and failed to climb Mount Everest, the highest mountain then known to man. Asked to speak a few weeks later, Edmund Hillary stood. He pointed towards the mountain and exclaimed "Mount Everest, you beat me the first time, but I'll beat you the next time because you've grown all you are going to grown . . . but I'm still growing!" One year later, Edmund Hillary became the first man to climb Mount Everest.

You are still growing. Get ready.

Faith leaves security and embraces surprise.

Verses 8–10 describe Abraham as one who "obeyed and went, even though he did not know where he was going." Abraham was wealthy and secure in his homeland. And if he remained there, he would have been as forgotten as all the others who were wealthy and secure with him (go ahead, name one of his wealthy neighbors). Instead, Abraham knew that to enter promise you must leave precedent.

I had started a church that was still well five years later. Attending a training event for pastors, I met a man who had started six churches and was working on another. I thought, "you're nuts." Later, during the session, I sensed the Lord say "You have another plant in you. Go and tell (my supervisor) now." I did. Turned out he was going that next weekend to a church to talk to them about their plans to start a daughter church. Yes, I planted and led the church. My family and I left everyone we knew and all the people we loved. But we started a church that would be the healthiest we've ever experienced.

After preaching a message, my habit is to pray and as I do so, to listen for any immediate application people might consider to

132   A Life Worth Becoming

the message. Once, I was praying and had the picture of a bridge, and I said "A bridge has been built for you. For some of you it is time to cross the bridge." Two of my closest friends told me afterwards they believed that was the Lord's encouragement to them. One started an auto business he had been considering but delaying, and the other started an embroidery business. Both were successful in their endeavors.

Is your name being called into terrains of the unfamiliar or less secure? Maybe ministry for you has been tightly controlled, planned by others, predictable and affirming; but now, you are being led into the more personal or anonymous, the spontaneous and new. Do you trust the God of surprise?

Eleanor Roosevelt said "You gain strength, courage and confidence by every experience in which you really stop to look fear in the face. You are able to say to yourself, "I have lived through this horror. I can take the next thing that comes along. You must do the thing you think you cannot do."

Faith gives away that God may give back.

Abraham offered Isaac as a sacrifice. Verse 19 reads "Abraham reasoned that God could raise the dead, and figuratively speaking, he did receive Isaac back from death."

God gives. He gives to us and in us that he might give through us. Abraham understood. He loved his son; he trusted his God. Faith gives because faith works.

I have a friend whose brother was about to lose everything. His tech stocks had bombed and his income and investments had soured. My friend said to him "I have $110,000.00. I'm single, you're not. The money is yours. You don't owe it to me." Two years later his brother repaid him in full. Cool brother. Cool faith.

Joseph   **133**

There are a couple of popular songs out right now in contemporary Christian music that assert "God gives and God takes away." I don't see that in the New Testament. I see that we can err, or sin and suffer consequence. I see that we can voluntarily give and therefore have less.

I don't see God taking, but I do see him giving. We don't give that He might give more. He gives, and then we give. He gives through us. That is why faith gives that God may give back—not as a financial investment plan, but as a conduit of his grace.

To listen to people preach about the tithe today you'd think pastor's are commission based sales reps. It isn't that difficult folks. The New Testament church gives because in Christ "God is able to make all grace abound to you, so that in all things at all times, having all that you need, you will abound in every good work. You will be made rich in every way so that you can be generous (how about more than 10%) on every occasion (2 Corinthians 8:8, 11)."

Faith gives. It gives out of opportunity not percentage. I had a guy tell me once, "I tried tithing, it doesn't work." I said, "You waste the 90%. Don't expect God to make up for it with 10%."

Whether it's time, energy or money, what God gives, we give, and he gives more that we might give more. As we pastor where we are, we will never open eyes more than in our giving. Generosity cuts against the grain of expectations and a me-first culture. Who needs what you have? The life worth becoming is extremely generous.

Faith speaks directive words at crossroads moments.

Hebrews 11:21–22 reads "By faith Jacob, when he was dying, blessed each of Joseph's sons . . . By faith Joseph, when his end was near, spoke about the exodus of the Israelites from Egypt."

134   A Life Worth Becoming

The practice of blessing gets lost in translation. We do know this: Jacob and Joseph gave voice to God's plan and promise, as had Isaac before them. Faith that chooses to listen is often asked to repeat what it heard. The words that follow are a gift, and they go to work.

Speaking is what I do. I have for years, and I don't intend to stop. When I teach or preach, it is as if God and I dance. It is our time.

But there are times he asks me to speak in a different context. I am to pass on to a person "blessing", to bring voice into their life. This is intimate. It feels as if I have been led into a person's bedroom where they and God alone dwell. I look around but it is not my place to become familiar.

These are tender times, adventurous times, and ominous times. Faith will lead you to speak into someone's life. It may come in the form of Scripture, advice or common sense. It may be dramatic (remember my dream with my high school friend) or seemingly offhand ("what do you have a God for"). Regardless, it is life-saving. There are two things to always remember when you speak.

First, just say what you "heard". I've had people pray for me, and I always tell them "just give me what you heard or saw, don't interpret." Why? God knows how to send a message, and we don't want to cloud it with our own understanding.

Second, don't hold back. I did once. A woman came to me for prayer, and as soon as she walked up a Bible reference came to me. I didn't know the verse by memory, and after she told me why she came I looked up the verse. She came to talk to me about her two boys; the verse specifically warned about calamity coming to two sons. I didn't give it to her. When she left, I felt a strong correction in my spirit. I promised God I would never do that again, and I haven't. I don't know what would have happened if I had shared it with her, but I know now I would have given it lovingly, and maybe that was the whole point of God's assignment.

Joseph

If we are going to be serious about *pastor where we are,* faith will lead us to speak a directive word. We can say it gently, without a lot of religious, churchy language, in a manner easy to understand, with love. But say it.

Faith grabs on, holds on and presses on.

When you read about Moses in verses 23–28, you see that his parents "saw he was no ordinary child" and they grabbed on to God's promise and disobeyed the king's edict. Moses, in turn, "chose to be mistreated along with the people of God . . . because he was looking ahead to his reward." He held on to God's promise and he pressed on through the dark night of the destroyer and the miraculous walls of the Red Sea.

One of my pastor-heroes, Ron Mehl, tells the following:

> I was fascinated recently to hear about a unique form of Chinese puppet theater. Mr. Yong Fong, a fifth-generation puppetry expert, explained that traditional, Chinese, hand-puppet theater is acted out on two levels at the same time.
>
> The lower level shows the characters as they progress moment by moment through the trial and tribulations of the play. On the upper lever, however, the audience can see how the play concludes, as the villains are punished and the heroes are rewarded. Because the audience can already see the outcome by looking up, they're not overly worried when the situation looks grave and the bad guys start to gain the upper hand. Instead, they get vocally involved. They begin shouting encouragement at the harried characters on the lower level. "Don't quit!" they'll shout. "Don't stop! Don't give up! We know you're going to make it!"

I prayed for a friend recently that his heart would be bigger than his vision. I'm all for vision! When you grab onto God's vision,

136　　　　A Life Worth Becoming

you must also have the heart that can hold on and press on through the trial and rejection.

Harriet Beacher Stowe said, "Never give up, for that is just the place and time that the tide will turn."

Charles Lindbergh would add, "Success is not measured by what a man accomplishes, but by the opposition he has encountered, and the courage with which he has maintained the struggle against overwhelming odds."

Are you feeling pressed in again? Have you said yes to the Lord's lead, but feel uncertain because others don't understand? Are questions and subtle accusations beginning to weigh you down? "Don't quit!"

Faith walks through a door another has opened.

Hebrews 11:29 is a beautiful verse, "By faith the people passed through the Red sea as on dry land." Who parted the Red Sea? God did. Whom did God use? Moses. Who passed through? The people of Israel. How did they pass? By faith.

We are so used to calling people to great faith in God's plan for their lives, we have done a disservice by not emphasizing times that faith follows the lead of another. There is no shame in following God's lead in a friend, family member or leader. As much as I contend that churches get away from celebrity leadership, still it is Biblical that God speaks to a whole through a few. That is why Hebrews 11:17 reads "Obey your leaders, submitting (the word authority per NIV is not in the Greek). They keep watch over you as men who must give an account. Obey them so that their work will be a joy, not a burden, for that would be of no advantage to you."

Joseph

Is there someone in your life leading out in a similar mission the Lord is entrusting to you? Is it possible he wants you to come alongside them first?

As a pastor, I committed myself to coaching people who wanted to start new ventures. For me, those times were like recess. One of the women I worked with wanted to start a ministry for teenage moms and dads. I was in the process of starting a new church, and she felt called to come alongside. She recognized that for her vision to be realized God was asking her to be a key part of the new church's vision. We grew together. A couple years later, and after I had moved, she wrote this letter:

> January 15, 2001
> Today Teen Parent Network officially took over the supervision of the DSHS tutoring. Without a single compromise of values, we are now a third party contractor with the state. There are 30 young mothers currently being tutored and before July, TPN will place tutors in the homes of probably 30 more families. I can only wonder at the lives that will change because of God's desires. Currently, 17 moms attend our weekly life skills group. We continue to provide transportation, child care, and food for these meetings. Everything is provided through volunteers. Our mom's have 25 children among themselves. We reach out to those children and to the grandparents of those children, and we even have people attend who are not young parents. They just want to come. By March we will have a short term child care facility in place and by May we will be operating The Hope Chest Clothing Boutique. By Fall, the vision is to have a Parent Enrichment Center in operation.
>
> Here are some stats on our clients. 100% of them are either working or in school. Two of them are in college!! 7 of them have given their lives to Christ and are regular church and Bible study attenders. The very first client we started with is marrying the father of her two children next month. The father is also a believer. He was baptized about two months ago. We have seen their lives

138   A Life Worth Becoming

change. And their two children are now going to be living in a real home where Jesus is worshipped. We have 9 clients who regularly attend our weekly Young Mom's Group. 25 volunteers are responsible for keeping this group provided with child care, transportation, and meals for the gals. It is amazing to me. We have mentors for 3 male clients now. How about that! God is doing great things and the prayer to serve our clients as well as volunteers is a reality.

She walked through a door others opened, until God led her into a room of her own.

Faith stands for the God who stands for you.

I love Rahab. The Bible says that by faith she welcomed the spies. Read the text in Joshua 2 and you see that she lied. She lied to protect the spies (here we go back to my class argument). How can the Bible call that faith? Rahab believed what she had heard about God, and though she did not know God, she showed kindness in response to those who followed God. She served to the best of her knowledge, even if her knowledge was limited and her service was short of truth (as opposed to Corrie Ten Boom, who knew God and served him in truth).

Years ago, Oswald was a young but very popular teacher with a growing ministry until a young woman came forward and pressed sexual charges against him. The village and surrounding areas believed the girl, and the young man was left devastated and with no opportunity to serve.

It was a lie. Regardless, his reputation shattered, the young man fought through the conflicting emotions of bitterness and doubt, forgiveness and faith. In the end, he chose to believe God, and God's promise in his life. He chose to believe that if he could give voice to truth, truth would prevail. And it has. Today, Oswald Chambers, and his book My Utmost For His Highest, continues to influence the lives of millions of followers of Christ.

Without faith, it is impossible to please God. With faith, the Spirit, prayer and word are dynamic, life-changing expressions within us and through us.

Free To Be

God sets you free. He has set you free in His Son. "It is for freedom that Christ has set us free."

He sets you free as sons. Jesus taught "I tell you the truth, everyone who sins is a slave to sin. Now a slave has no permanent place in the family, but a son belongs to it forever. So if the Son sets you free, you will be free indeed."

You are free in His Spirit—"Now the Lord is the Spirit, and where the Spirit of the Lord is, there is freedom."

The word for freedom means the ability to go where ever. God sets you free so that you are able to go where he leads. You are free to become.

No Law But Him

For sin shall not be your master, because you are not under law, but under grace . . . though you used to be slaves to sin, you have been set free from sin and have become slaves to righteousness.

What does it mean we are not under law? Paul clarified that "To those under the law I became like one under the law (though I myself am not under the law), so as to win those under the law. To

140   A Life Worth Becoming

those not having the law I became like one not having the law (though I am not free from God's law but am under Christ's law) so as to win those not having the law."

The Christian is not under any law but Christ. "Christ is the end of law," Paul declared. "Okay", someone will ask, "But what about the Old Testament and the Jewish moral law. We still have to obey the Ten Commandments don't we?"

Put On Your Thinking Caps

John 1:17 says, "For the law was given through Moses; grace and truth came through Jesus Christ."

Jesus came not to destroy the law but to fulfill it. He did fulfill it, and when he cried out "It is finished" on the cross he used a word meaning *paid in full.* He fulfilled the law as a Promissory Note is fulfilled when paid or when a set of blueprints are fulfilled at the completion of the house. He lived the life the law prescribed. He paid the penalty the law required. He upheld it and he nailed it to the cross.

- Before this faith came, we were held prisoners by the law, locked up until faith should be revealed. So the law was put in charge to lead us to Christ that we might be justified by faith. Now that faith has come, we are no longer under the supervision of the law. Galatians 3:23–25
- But if you are led by the Spirit, you are not under law. Galatians 5:18
- So, my brothers, you also died to the law through the body of Christ . . . but now, dying to what once bound us, we have been released from the law so that we serve in the new way of the Spirit, and not in the old way of the written code. Romans 7:4,6

Joseph
141

- The former regulation is set aside because it was weak and useless (for the law made nothing perfect), and a better hope is introduced, by which we draw near to God. Hebrews 7:18,19

The law of Christ is Christ-likeness. It is renewal in his image. Not only is Christ the end of law, he is the definition and embodiment of morality. As a result, man's need for moral direction and a moral objective is summed up in Christ. His word is our authority and his life is our code.

Therefore, Paul would warn us against spiritual bullies who seek to impose any law or moral ethic beyond that of Christ.

- Watch out for those dogs, those men who do evil, those mutilators of the flesh. Philippians 3:2
- See to it that no one takes you captive through hollow and deceptive philosophy, which depends on human tradition and the basic principles of this world rather than on Christ . . . Therefore, do not let anyone judge you by what you eat or drink, or with regard to a religious festival . . . Since you died with Christ to the basic principles of this world, why, as though you still belonged to it, do you submit to its rules: Do not handle! Do not taste! Do not touch! Colossians 2:16, 20–21

Those who live free do not use their freedom to indulge the sinful nature, nor do they use their freedom to cause another to stumble (a weaker brother, not a bully). Instead, recognizing they belong to the Lord, they live to the Lord.

But it takes courage to live freely.

Several generations ago, during one of the most turbulent of the desert wars in the Middle East, a spy was captured and sentenced to death by a general of the Persian army. The general, a

142 A Life Worth Becoming

man of intelligence and compassion, had adopted a strange and unusual custom in such cases. He permitted the condemned person to make a choice. The prisoner could either face the firing squad or pass through the Black Door.

As the moment of the execution drew near, the general ordered the spy to be brought before him for a short, final interview, the primary purpose of which was to receive the answer of the doomed man to the query: "What shall it be—the firing squad or the Black Door?"

This was not an easy decision and the prisoner hesitated, but soon made it known that he much preferred the firing squad to the unknown horrors that might await him behind the ominous and mysterious door. Not long thereafter, a volley of shots in the courtyard announced that the grim sentence had been fulfilled.

The general, staring at his boots, turned to his aide and said, "You see how it is with men; they will always prefer the known way to the unknown. It is characteristic of people to be afraid of the undefined. Yet I gave him his choice."

"What lies beyond the Black Door?" asked the aide. "Freedom," replied the general, "and I've known only a few brave enough to take it."

"It is for freedom that Christ has set us free. Stand firm, then, and do not let yourselves be burdened again by a yoke of slavery."

People fear our freedom. They will attempt in all sorts of religious ways to corral our freedom. They will argue, intimidate and manipulate. According to them, we'll need to "come under authority, get on the same page, show humility, model submission". What they really want is for us to be like them than like Christ. Our freedom threatens them, stretches them and challenges them. If we change, they might need to change. If we are different, their sameness might be more apparent.

Don't you just want to live by the Bible? Wouldn't it be nice to just need to be more like Jesus? Do we really need all this leadership development in order to be visionaries, apostles, prophets,

Joseph

pastors, warriors, commanders, and more? Do I have to take yet another class to learn even more acronyms so that I can live an abundant life? How did Jesus teach without acronyms anyway?

I'm not a big fan of bullies. I learned the hard way how they steal your joy. When I was in seventh grade there was a giant in ninth grade whose last name was Masterjohn. I always heard it as Master John. He liked the desserts my mom would send with my lunch, so anytime he saw me he would demand my snack. I lost out on some good dessert. One day I had enough. I told him "No". Do you know what he did? Nothing. Apparently he only bullied those who let him.

God has done something amazing in your life. In the person of Jesus he has saved you, and with the presence of his Spirit he fills you. You are no longer defined by circumstance or dominated by criticism. You are free. You are free to rise above it all. You can go anywhere, because where God leads, you follow, and no one gets in his way. You actually walk in step with his Spirit, partnering with him in prayer, shaped by his word. Sin will not stop you. Law cannot condemn you.

Bullies, step aside!

Edward Woodman took his two children, 11-year old David and 8-year old Elizabeth out on their boat.

Elizabeth, spotting some driftwood in the water, reached out with a fish net to pick it up. The drag of the wood in the net pulled her over, and she hit the prop hard. The blades tore into her right arm and tangled in the material from her sweater.

When the engine stopped, Woodman walked to the stern and saw his daughter trapped below. He dove in and tried to free Elizabeth but without success. Surfacing, he called to David, "I have to keep giving her air!"

David prayed, "Please God, don't let her die." Then he remembered the knife.

144   A Life Worth Becoming

When his father surfaced again, David pulled out his pocketknife.

Woodman could only cut away so much material without getting to close to her wounded arm.

His fingers tugged at the remaining material but it was unyielding. He wrestled with the propeller but it wouldn't budge.

Finally, Woodman cut some more, as close to her arm as possible. He braced his feet against the prop and pulled with all he had.

Elizabeth came free!

When Woodman signed his daughter into the hospital, he could barely hold the pen. The blades had cut into his palm and fingers.

Later, a reporter asked Elizabeth if she had been afraid.

"Oh, I knew my daddy would save me," she said, "And he did."

The life worth becoming lives by faith, freely! Our Father has saved us. You can rest assured that God knows how to make you, and he does so outside of any formula or system man might put forth, even with the best of intentions.

To become like Christ we must follow the lead of the Spirit, and he has a habit of walking wherever he wants.

I Will Trust Love

I told my oldest daughter two things before she left for college. The first was "I repent." I had joked when she was young that when she turned 18 she was out of the house. That was a stupid joke. Instead, I got on my knees and begged her to not leave.

The second thing I said was "trust love." I told her that she was going to meet a lot of people, some she would naturally like and others not so easily, but that regardless now was the time to see what happens when one simply loves.

Trust love is one of the last things Jesus said before he left. "A new command I give you," he shared with his followers, "Love one another. By this will all men know that you are my disciples, if you love one another."

Love. When I was a young preacher I used to be a fireball on topics like evangelism, commitment, obedience, warfare and anything juicy for debate. Then one day my father asked me, "When am I going to hear you preach about love?" He didn't intend for it to be an offhand remark, and I didn't take it that way. I've been on a journey with love ever since.

The life worth becoming is characterized by grace, friendship and innovation. These three are first cultivated in our life as we experience personal transformation: As we become more like Jesus. We become more like him as we interact with God through his Spirit. We relate with God through prayer and devotion to his word, walking freely by faith. But personal transformation isn't the only means by which we develop grace, friendship and innovation.

God has made us for relationship. Since God is in himself community—Father, Son and Spirit—to be made in his image is to be relational. It is to love. To this end, God sees salvation not only as deliverance from sin but restoration of relationship, both with him and between each other.

I used to gloss over Ephesians 2:11–22. It seemed to follow the good stuff and required extra time and attention to understand it. Then one day I gave it the attention it deserved. What a cool passage!

In verses 11–13, Paul is basically saying that at one point, the nation of Israel and those outside of it were as separated as could be. The term uncircumcised is literally translated *foreskin* and was a derogatory term. Instead of competing in games as shirts and skins, they competed as—well, you get the point. Excluded from citizenship meant a person had no legal rights, and worse they had no claim to promises of God ("without hope"). The idea of being far away originally referred to distance from Jerusalem. In other words, Gentiles were on the wrong team (the foreskins), shut out from legal rights, divine promises and the city of God.

But through Christ all are brought near. Peace, the harmony and security found in right relationship, is shared in him. Verses 14–22 teach that Jesus destroyed "the barrier, the dividing wall of hostility." The barrier was a fence signifying protection, and the dividing wall described the separation of the court of the Gentiles form the temple proper. One inscription on the wall read "No foreigner may enter within the barricade which surrounds the sanctuary and enclosure. Anyone who is caught doing so will have himself to blame for his ensuing death." That takes "No Trespassing" to new levels, doesn't it?

Jesus destroyed it by "abolishing in his flesh the law with its commandments and regulations." The word "abolish" means to make ineffective or powerless.

Instead, he made one new man out of two and "through him we both have access to the Father by one Spirit." The word "access" refers to a stage in which an official in court would conduct visitors into the king's presence. Notice in this verse the role of the Son, Father and Spirit. God is in himself community.

We are no longer foreigners (transients) and aliens (residents without rights). We are fellow citizens, members of the household, a holy temple together. We are the beautiful bride.

Salvation is not just about God and me. It is about God and us. The Bible is clear. I cannot love God, whom I haven't seen, if I don't love you, who I do see—at your best and at your worst. Jesus prayed movingly in John 17 for our unity in relationship. Our togetherness was worth praying for—and dying for.

There are two words in popular use today that describe the importance of relationship. One is the biblical word fellowship. The Greek word, *koinonia,* was used outside the New Testament to speak of an unbroken bond between the gods and men, and of the bond between men themselves. Paul's emphasis on the word was the unique relationship between a believer and God. Acts 2:42 says the early church devoted themselves to "the fellowship", and John says we have fellowship with one another. Fellowship speaks of what is held in common, of partnership and unbreakable bond.

A contemporary word similar in meaning is community. Obviously, the idea of *common* is easily seen in the word.

Businesses today have *communities of practice.* These are groups who share similar issues and expand their knowledge and increase their skill by ongoing interaction. Along the way, they develop relationships and identifiable patterns of behavior. The most effective communities welcome strong personalities and are unafraid of disagreement or controversy, understanding that sharpening one another results in greater vitality.

The church has been reclaiming the beauty of community. Gilbert Bilezikian has written a book titled *Community 101* that has served as a premier theological premise for experiencing oneness.

A Life Worth Becoming

In his book *Connecting,* Dr. Larry Crabb, the renowned psychotherapist and Christian author, passionately argues for the healing to be found in Christians genuinely connecting with each other. He writes:

> I have strong reason to suspect that Christians sitting dutifully in church congregations, for whom "going to church" means doing a variety of spiritual activities, have been given resources that if released could powerfully heal broken hearts, overcome the damage done by abusive backgrounds, encourage the depressed to move courageously forward, stimulate the lonely to reach out, revitalize discouraged teens and children with new and holy energy, and introduce hope into the lives of the countless people who feel rejected, alone, and useless. Maybe "going to church", more than anything else, means relating to several people in your life differently. *Maybe the center of Christian community is connecting with a few* (italics his).

Bingo.

Intentional relationship is proactive love. The word intentional describes the priority and manner of our relationship. Unless I am intentional, circumstances, tiredness and personality traits can cause me to lose the experience of community I seek. That's a nice way of saying that I can be lazy and easily distracted.

We all have natural networks of relationship. They are people we interact with on a regular basis, whether it is through family, neighborhood, work or activity. They are also people God has entrusted to us. In the midst of all the people we know, some have been deliberately placed in our life by God. They are precious people that the Lord has determined will be touched by him through us. We are called to pastor them, whether they are many or few, following Christ or not.

The question is, "What does intentional relationship look like?" What will characterize our relationship with people we are

Joseph

called to love purposefully? If we search the Bible for stories and examples that answer the question, we notice that intentional relationship is characterized by protection, provision and participation. We make a difference in the lives of others when we are there for them, giving to them, sharing with them.

I Am For You

Paul penned the classic verse "Love is patient, love is kind. It does not envy, it does not boast, it is not proud." These are words of acceptance. I love you right where you are, good and bad, seen and unseen, the pleasing and the annoying.

Because love is patient, I see the best in you. The word patient speaks of a person who is wronged but will not exercise his power to avenge. God is this way to us. Peter wrote "He is patient with you, not wanting anyone to perish, but everyone to come to repentance . . . Bear in mind that our Lord's patience means salvation."

When I try your patience, your love does not assume my momentary character is the sum of who I am or could be. Instead, you see the best in me, the possibility of what might be. You choose to see what others overlook, at times revealing to me what I don't even see in myself. You remember I am growing, and your patience reminds me of the same.

The Bible character Lot doesn't make a great first impression when he appears in Scripture. We first meet him after God calls Abram to leave everything, and one of those who accompany him is his nephew Lot. We don't know much about Lot until Genesis 13 when Abram gives him a choice of land to settle in. Lot will go one way, Abram the other. Lot looks around and picks the good land for himself. It seems a bit selfish at first reading. Frankly, Lot will make a few decisions we shake our head at.

150　　　　　　　A Life Worth Becoming

But Abram sees the best in Lot. So, after Lot is captured, the Bible says Abram gathered 318 trained men, attacked, and recovered all the goods stolen together with the women and other people, including Lot. In 2 Peter, Lot will be described as a righteous man; Abram saw something in Lot beyond his poor decision making.

Love not only sees the best *in another,* it wants the best *for another.* That's why love is kind. The word was used in the Old Testament to spotlight God's abundant goodness. When someone wants the best for another, they believe that the other's success is their own success. It is why Abram would give Lot first choice of land, and why he would risk his life to recover Lot's.

Love protects. It says "I am for you", and therefore "I will fight for you". Intentional relationship is not weak. When God's people were being threatened when they rebuilt the walls of Jerusalem, Nehemiah stood and said "Don't be afraid of them. Remember the Lord, who is great and awesome, and fight for your brothers. . . . From that day on, half of my men did the work, while the other half were equipped with spears, shields, bows and armor."

Who knows you are for them? Who knows you see the best in them and want the best for them, that you will fight for them?

My daughters love to tell the story of when they were very young and playing out in the front yard. I was watching from inside the house when I noticed the bully girl next door starting to shove one of mine. I bolted out of the house and yelled for her to stop. Everyone froze. It was a simple moment, but one of my girls has said it taught them that I would always come to their rescue. (At that point I showed them how to defend themselves, including how to grab a person so they couldn't get away. It was a funny day when I saw my daughter yelling for her friend to slow down so she could grab her).

Paul contrasts acceptance with envy. Envy says "I don't want you to have what you have." It is the opposite of kind and protective love. Why do I succumb to envy? A person's best may seem bet-

Joseph 151

ter than my best. So, I become boastful and proud. I keep you at a distance so that you do not see my weakness. This would be King Saul. In I Samuel 18, women were dancing and singing acclaim to David. The Bible says "Saul was very angry; 'They have credited David with tens of thousands,' he thought, 'but me with only thousands. What more can he get but the kingdom?' And from that time on Saul kept a jealous eye on David."

God has placed people in our life who need to know we are for them. We see the best in them and want the best for them. Again, who is that for you?

As a result, "Love always protects, always trusts, always hopes, always perseveres." The idea of protects is "cover".

When I am for you, I am alongside you. And I've got you covered. My lips won't reveal your faults nor repeat your sins. My strengths will balance your weakness. My forgiveness will void your error. My presence will serve notice that your enemy will have to deal with more than you.

In Genesis 21:22, the commanders of forces said to Abraham "God is with you in everything you do. Now swear to me here before God that you will not deal falsely with me or my children . . . Abraham said, "I swear it." He had them covered.

When I am for you, I understand that love trusts. Please notice that this verse does not necessarily say love trusts a person.

One of my favorite moments in youth ministry was during a game of capture the flag. The object of the game is two teams trying to get flags at opposite ends of a course. The flag is guarded by one person, and if you are tagged by any of the opposing team while trying to get the flag you are a prisoner of war. I love to win. So, while everyone else was figuring out how to maneuver, I went up to the guard, pulled out some money and bribed him to let me have the flag. There is nothing in the rules that says you can't bribe the guard. Some of my staff didn't quite appreciate my cunning.

152   A Life Worth Becoming

There is an interesting verse in John 2:24, 25 "But Jesus would not entrust himself to them, for he knew all men. He did not need man's testimony about man, for he knew what was in a man."

If Jesus didn't trust man, are we called to trust one another? Since the word trust conveys *putting one's full weight upon* something, the answer is obviously "no." I don't ask people to trust me, because I am subject to circumstances beyond my control that can affect my promise or intent. God is above circumstance and sin; he can be trusted. So when love trusts, it trusts the God who is working in and around another. I am for you, and therefore, I trust God in you over the long road we share.

When the apostle Paul, then named Saul, first tried to join the disciples they were afraid of him because of his past persecution of the church. "But Barnabas took him and brought him to the apostles. He told them how Saul on his journey had seen the Lord and that the Lord had spoken to him, and how in Damascus he had preached fearlessly in the name of Jesus. So Saul stayed with them and moved about freely in Jerusalem." Barnabas trusted the Lord of intervention.

Because I am for you, I understand that love hopes. Hope measures differently. I am alongside you for the duration because life is measured against the eternal, not the immediate. Failure is not final and success is not forever. Love is forever, and I measure you not because of value you might bring to our relationship, but simply because of whom you are and who God will make you to be. The worth you bring is already established in the cross you bear.

Love perseveres. The word means to *bear up* and is active, not passive. In other words, I don't simply hang on in relationship with you, but together we press into all that is intended for you. We put on the shoulder pads and I block for you. Pity the defender who gets in our way.

Joseph   **153**

Forgiveness is central if I am for you and will come alongside you. Through it all, you and I will fail. We will disappoint the other. We will intend one thing and do another. We will promise and not keep our word. We will sin.

When I trained church planters on how to write a mission statement, almost everyone would write how their church was a safe place. I would say "You can't write that. You will not be a safe place. You will be a place with people and they will sin. You can be a place where you seek to forgive together and heal together, but it will not be safe. You would be more accurate to guarantee that people will be hurt and disappointed. But they will also be extraordinarily loved through their failures and through your own."

I smile when people argue we need to get back to being like the New Testament church. I point out that most of the letters to the church were written to correct false beliefs and sinful behavior, and that churches then were full of manipulation, conceit, backbiting and selfishness. "I think we are already like the New Testament church", I respond. "What we want is to be the beautiful bride."

Because you are for me and alongside me, you forgive me. Paul says there are two signs of an offended heart: To be rude and to be self-seeking. We think of rude as being "not nice". It really means to objectify. Let's say I'm driving down the road and you cut me off. I will likely think, in the middle of singing to the worship CD I have playing in the car, "You jerk." But what if I noticed you next to me first and recognized you were my friend. Down the road you cut me off. I think, "Wow, friend, you must still need to wake up". In the first instance, you are an object, an unknown, and I name you Jerk. In the second, I know you, and you are not an object of derision but a friend, and I name you Forgiven.

I was rude when the televangelist scandals of the 1980s hit. I remember saying to my friends about Jim Bakker and the others

154   A Life Worth Becoming

that if they were sincere in their ministry, they would find ways to minister out of the spotlight after the scandal blew over. Not many years after I was reading a book by Tony Campolo in which he shared how Jim Bakker ministered to inmates while he was in prison. I wept as I read, and through the tears asked God to forgive me for my judgment and ignorance. And Jim, I'm sorry.

An offended heart is self-seeking. It insists on one's rights. When I am offended, I pull back. My giving is less sizable. You expect a birthday present from me and you get a card.

Paul says the safeguard against offense is love that is not easily angered and keeps no record of wrong. I am not easily angered when I see the big picture. I keep someone's error in perspective, and give more weight to our relationship than to their failure. When God says he will remember our sins no more, do you really think it means he forgets, as in cannot remember? It means that he refuses to call a past failure into the present, and refuses to allow it to define the relationship, to be a block between what is and what will be.

Friends need forgiveness. We experience the beauty of intentional relationship when people know we see their best and want their best. They know we are there to protect them, and to be alongside them for the distance despite the disappointments along the way.

Who needs that from you today?

Real Love Freely Gives

Intentional relationship practices God's economy: God gives. To love others is to trust in God's provision and to provide for others in turn. Rather than hold on or hold back, love believes that God's provision is greater than what we can acquire on our own.

Joseph

It is why Biblical giving is enthusiastic and extravagant. Paul said "Each man should give what he has decided in his heart to give, not reluctantly or under compulsion, for God loves a cheerful giver." In the Old Testament we see "The people rejoiced at the willing response of the leaders, for they had given freely and wholeheartedly to the Lord". People gave so much once Moses had to restrain them from giving more.

Giving expresses love for each other and for God. Paul described the Philippians' giving as a fragrant offering and acceptable sacrifice, the same terminology used elsewhere to describe the sacrifice of Christ, as well as worship, evangelism and good works.

The Bible is clear on what we are to give to. We give taxes. We give to family. We give to people in need. We give what we have and we give ourselves. We give because we trust God; we believe that we cannot out give God.

Abram believed it. He gave Lot the choice of land. Hagar believed it. When Sarai mistreated her, she fled. The angel of the Lord found her and told her "Go back to your mistress and submit to her. I will so increase your descendants that they will be too numerous to count." Real love freely gives one's self, not just possessions.

Israel learned it. They were told that at the end of every seven years they were to cancel debts. David taught it to his army at the division of the spoils. He commanded, "The share of the man who stayed with the supplies is to be the same as that of him who went down to the battle. All will share alike." Nehemiah intervened and demanded "Let the exacting of usury stop! Give back to them immediately their fields, vineyards and houses, and also the usury you are charging them." Generosity includes fair dealing.

The early church practiced giving in relationship:

> All the believers were together and had everything in common. Selling their possessions and goods, they gave to anyone as he had need.

156   A Life Worth Becoming

> All the believers were one in heart and mind. No one
> claimed that any of his possessions was his own, but they shared
> everything they had.

No where in the text is there indication that this was a new economic structure for everyone and for all-time. Instead, it was the generous response of the church in the right time for people in need.

Notice a beautiful act of giving in Acts 18:5 "When Silas and Timothy came from Macedonia, Paul devoted himself exclusively to preaching." Before they came, Paul had to work to support himself. Upon their coming, they worked in order to generously give to Paul the gift of time. They were one in community.

I remember one of my ministry coaches approaching me. They wanted to give the gift of a cleaning service to one of our leaders who had been so busy the house had been neglected. They wondered if it was a good idea and if it could be done tactfully. I said it was beautiful, and I knew the love would outweigh the awkwardness. The leader was extremely grateful for the gift.

When we give to people we give to God. A gift to a person is as valuable, right and honored as a check in the offering plate. I dare anyone to Biblically show me otherwise. "A generous man will prosper; he who refreshes others will himself be refreshed." God has given into your life people who need to be refreshed.

Today my junior high son took a friend to a bookstore and bought him a Bible. Did that move the heart of God as much as when my son puts money in the offering bag?

A friend of mine was a broke Bible College student, crying one day alone in his room and considering leaving school. He received $50.00 that day from a secret friend. My friend told me that gift was enough to help push him off the bed and keep going.

Who needs refreshing? Who needs something you have? Who needs you? Henry Wadsworth Longfellow said "Give what you have to some one, it may be better than you dare to think."

Joseph

157

Try something this week. Leave a ridiculously large tip. Buy someone's meal at a restaurant. See that person behind you in the coffee drive-thru? When you pay for yours, leave enough to cover their drink too. Take some money and give it to one of your seeking friends. Tell them to be nice to themselves. Refresh someone!

All Together Now

The third dynamic of intentional relationship is participation. Life is lived together, from the simplest acts to the most meaningful. Acts 1:4 records "On one occasion, while he was eating with them, he gave them this command." We frequently see references of Jesus eating with people. The early church "broke bread in their homes and ate together with glad and sincere hearts".

We participate with our friends in four ways. Love hangs out, ministers to, teams with and shares in.

If there is one thing I would like to see in Scripture more than is recorded it is the times Jesus would hang out with his disciples. We get glimpses. We see them at a wedding together. "After this he went down to Capernaum with his mother and brothers and his disciples. There they stayed for a few days." Don't you want to know what happened? Many of Jesus' parables were inspired at moments in which they were simply doing something in the normal course of another day. There weren't a lot of staged events and intricate planning to his ministry. It happened in the course of living together.

I have a friend I haven't seen for awhile. We experienced a lot together. We moved out of state to Bible College, married while in school, started families close together, commiserated over early ministry experiences, led a church together, irritated people together. There is a lot of *together* in our relationship. And the memories I have best are playing football, early morning breakfasts, skipping chapel services and spontaneous, crazy acts of serving people unexpectedly. Our most meaningful conversations always happened at these times, behind the curtain.

Play was also the first thing to go when we were mad at each other. We could still conduct services and "minister" on the platform, but when we were deep in disagreement we didn't play or eat together, and we distanced ourselves from the spontaneous. There may be a clue here: *What is most valuable becomes the most vulnerable when a relationship is strained.*

Believe in the daily. Work the simple. The dress rehearsals, in which people blow their lines and laugh together, is what draws the actors close. The performance entertains, but the practices bond. You have friends with whom you need to practice more, realizing Christ-like ministry may be found here more than when the curtain rises.

One of my best memories as a dad is when I worked a job that would often allow me home by late afternoon to watch with my two young daughters the cartoon Chip 'n Dale Rescue Rangers. I would be in the middle with them on either side, and we would sing the opening song and make comments throughout the show. You can't replace just hanging out.

My oldest daughter was required to conduct a senior project before she graduated from high school. It involved a set number of hours of actual service, a written report and a presentation. She chose to host a group that met weekly in our home. It was comprised of a dozen of her student friends, half of whom embraced faith and half who did not. The rules were simple: Meet regularly, talk openly of real life issues, and respect each others' perspective. If someone offended another, they worked it out on the spot. They had some great meetings. But the real ministry took place before and after the discussion time, around the billiards table upstairs and the kitchen downstairs. Their laughter still echoes off our walls.

Go ahead. Expand that room you've always been talking about and buy the pool table. Life happens after the break.

Minister To

Spiritual gifts are relational. If you look at the list of gifts, it is hard to build programs around them. I love and appreciate the "platform gifts". I've spent all of my adult life preaching and speaking to large groups. I am grateful for the platform, and have been inspired by the teaching leadership and worship leadership I have received from others who are gifted for public ministry. But most gifts are far more personal in their expression.

> We have different gifts according to the grace given us. If a man's gift is prophesying, let him use it in proportion to his faith. If it is serving, let him serve; if it is teaching, let him teach; if it is encouraging, let him encourage; if it is contributing to the needs of others, let him give generously; if it is leadership, let him govern diligently; if it is showing mercy, let him do it cheerfully.

We've seen these programmed into the church. But what if these gifts are primarily expressed personally? For instance, Paul wrote that a person might have the gift of contributing to the needs of others. The church has you give an offering, and affirms that you are exercising your spiritual gift of giving. It seems to me that this verse speaks more to giving to the need of another, a real live person with flesh and breath. And what about encouraging? Or mercy? These are spontaneous acts to meet immediate need.

A Life Worth Becoming

The Bible says there are certain things we do for "one another". Here is the list:

1. be devoted
2. honor
3. do not judge
4. build up
5. accept
6. admonish
7. care for
8. serve
9. bear the burdens of
10. be patient
11. be kind
12. speak to
13. forgive
14. teach
15. comfort
16. encourage
17. stir to love and good works
18. confess sins to
19. pray
20. show hospitality

The spiritual gifts listed in Scripture are what God does through us to accomplish these (See I Corinthians 12, Romans 12 and I Peter 4). The Bible doesn't tell us to discover our spiritual gift. It tells us to serve people.

How do we know God will empower us to meet their need? He led them to us in the first place. He might have a plan. Trust love.

When I coach people on relational, lifestyle ministry, I help them do three things for people: pray for them, encourage them and resource them.

In the chapter on prayer we considered different ways to hear God on behalf of people. But what is happening as we hear and as

Joseph   161

we communicate? The Bible uses different words to convey the gifts being given: word of wisdom, word of knowledge, prophecy, tongues. When we pray, we are in partnership with the Holy Spirit for the sake of our friend, and we need the Spirit to tell us things we do not know and lead us in ways we do not see. The gifts are relational and personal.

Barnabas was called the Son of Encouragement. We are never more an agent of the Holy Spirit (also called Helper) than when we come alongside another to help and encourage. Consider the gifts named to this end: encouraging, contributing, mercy, faith, help.

People we love have goals and aspirations. At times, they need help in realizing the resources at their disposal. Sometimes those resources are within them, and at other times outside of them. We love our friend when we reveal resources of his own or connect him with the resources of others. It is possible we are a resource. And so the Bible speaks of gifts of teaching, contributing, leading, healing, discerning of spirits and administration. At times, we fill what is lacking. If we cannot, we help our friend find one who can.

The life worth becoming is one that sees the success of another as their success. Jesus came to serve, not to be served. God has entrusted to us people who need someone to come alongside and minister to them. In *The American Scholar Magazine,* Wyatt Prunty captured this dynamic.

LEARNING THE BICYCLE
(for Heather)

The older children pedal past
Stable as little gyros, spinning hard
To supper, bath, and bed, until at last
We also quit, silent and tired
Beside the darkening yard where trees

162   A Life Worth Becoming

Now shadow up instead of down.
Their predictable lengths can only tease
Her as, head lowered, she walks her bike alone
Somewhere between her wanting to ride
And her certainty she will always fall.
Tomorrow, though I will run behind,
Arms out to catch her, she'll tilt then balance wide
Of my reach, till distance makes her small,
Smaller, beyond the place I stop and know
That to teach her I had to follow
And when she learned I had to let her go.

When you are my friend, I want to hang out with you and minister to you. I also want to serve with you.

Team With

God loves teams. The Father, Son and Spirit are teamed together (I'm on their side). Moses teamed with Aaron, Elijah teamed with Elisha, Jonathan teamed with David, and Jesus teamed with his disciples. Though the emphasis of this book is on individuals in relational, lifestyle ministry, a critical component of a life worth becoming is shared ministry. No one is called to serve alone. And though the church has become overly dependent upon program ministry (no matter what they call it), there will never be a day in which the church does not express its life in the form of people working together toward a common good.

No matter whom I love, the fullness of Christ's beauty is not seen in me alone. It is seen with me in relationship with others whose gifts and experiences provide a more complete tapestry.

There are at least five reasons we team with people.

Joseph

1. Serving together we strengthen each other. Our works of service is "so that the body of Christ may be built up . . . From him the whole body grows and builds itself up in love as each part does its work."

2. The need is too great for one alone. Moses father-in-law told him "What you are doing is not good. You and these people who come to you will only wear yourselves out. The work is too heavy for you; you cannot handle it alone . . . But select capable men from all the people . . . have them bring every difficult case to you; the simple cases they can decide themselves." Jesus said "The harvest is plentiful but the workers are few."
As a teen I heard someone say "People say I would rather burn out than rust out—but either way you're out!"

3. It takes an army to win a war. Because we talk about ministry in the context of love, it is easy to forget that ministry is also battle. We decisively intervene in Satan's attempt to steal, kill and destroy another. Instead, we are God's voice to correct deception and God's hands to deliver from trial. Jesus "called his twelve disciples to him and gave them authority to drive out evil spirits and to heal every disease and sickness, and "appointed seventy-two others and sent them two by two ahead of him to every town and place where he was about to go."

4. We believe each other well. Barnabas contended for Saul when others feared him. He would later contend for Mark when Paul was frustrated with him. When we serve with each other, we affirm what God can do in the other.

A Life Worth Becoming

I love you,
Not only for what you are,
But for what I am
When I am with you.

I love you,
Not only for what
You have made of yourself,
But for what
You are making of me.

I love you
For the part of me
That you bring out;
I love you
For putting your hand
Into my heaped-up heart
And passing over
All the foolish, weak things
That you can't help
Dimly seeing there,
And for drawing out
Into the light
All the beautiful belongings
That no one else had looked
Quite far enough to find.

I love you because you
Are helping me to make
Of the lumber of my life
Not a tavern
But a temple;
Out of the works

Joseph 165

Of my every day
Not a reproach
But a song.
—Roy Croft, quoted in Hazel Felleman, *The Best Loved Poems of the American People*

5. We pass the baton. We are the third leg of the relay, setting up the fourth leg for victory. Jesus told his disciples "go and make disciples of all nations, baptizing them in the name of the Father and of the Son and of the Holy Spirit, and teaching them to obey everything I have commanded you." Paul instructed young Timothy, "What you heard from me, keep as the pattern of sound teaching, with faith and love in Christ Jesus. Guard the good deposit that was entrusted to you . . . And the things you heard me say I the presence of many witnesses entrust to reliable men who will also be qualified to teach others."

Passing the baton is both intentional and natural. Paul tells Timothy to teach, and we also see the disciples learn as they go.

Share In

The life worth becoming is intentional about learning and worshiping with others.

Jesus said "I no longer call you servants, because a servant does not know his master's business. Instead, I have called you friends, for everything that I learned from my Father I have made known to you." This is the truth that drives my learning with another. I don't learn with people for the sake of knowledge alone. I seek to learn what Christ is making known.

166   A Life Worth Becoming

Jesus modeled this with the disciples. At the end of Matthew 9 Jesus is going through the villages preaching and healing. Jesus led the disciples and did the ministry. In Matthew 10, the disciples are sent to preach and heal. Jesus led but the disciples did the ministry. In the end of Matthew, Jesus sends his disciples into the world. The disciples are leading and doing. They learned what Christ had made known, and in his continued presence as the risen Savior they continued to learn

Learning is both general and situational. Generally, the early church was devoted to the apostle's teaching. They met regularly to learn often the truth of the Scriptures. In Acts 11, though, you have a different learning modeled. A dispute arose because Peter went into the house of uncircumcised men and ate with them. The text says in verse 4 that Peter explained everything to them precisely as it had happened. The result is recorded in verse 18 "When they heard this, they had no further objections and praised God." A group was without understanding, and they learned together through Peter that God was taking the gospel to Gentiles. In this sense, we learn together not a specific theology or set of truths, but we learn how God is moving in the world and fleshing out applications of those truths.

What does relational, lifestyle ministry look like? How do we pastor believing and unbelieving friends? What does a church do to transition from program-based, personality-centered ministry to a coaching movement of lifestyle ministers? These are the questions we learn together.

Intentional relationships also worship together. Worship has always been a priority in relationship with God. God set aside days for the sole purpose of worship: "Do no work at all on these days, except to prepare food for everyone to eat—that is all you may do . . . Celebrate this day as a lasting ordinance for the generations to come."

Joseph

People responded to the Lord with worship. Moses and the Israelites sang this song to the Lord: "I will sing to the Lord, for he is highly exalted." Later, Israel "took an oath to the Lord with loud acclamation, with shouting and with trumpets and horns. All Judah rejoiced about the oath because they had sworn it wholeheartedly. They sought God eagerly, and he was found by them."

Worship is the baton we pass. Judges 2:10–11 sadly read "After that whole generation had been gathered to their fathers, another generation grew up, who knew neither the Lord nor what he had done for Israel." How could that be? Mom and Dad didn't worship.

We worship because we recognize it is there that the battle is won. When Israel was threatened, King Hezekiah and Isaiah cried out in prayer to heaven "And the Lord sent an angel, who annihilated all the fighting men and the leaders and officers in the camp of the Assyrian king." Ironically, the king went into the temple of his god, and some of his sons killed him there. The Lord saved Hezekiah in response to his worship; the king of Assyria was killed in worship to his false god.

The battle is won in worship because we see God for who he is and see our circumstances with right perspective: God is good and great, and our circumstances are temporal and passing. When we worship together, we remind each other of who God is and how God delivers.

The Holy Spirit interacts with our worship. "They were filled with the Holy Spirit and spoke the word of God boldly." On one occasion "Agabus, stood up and through the Spirit predicted that a severe famine would spread over the entire Roman world." Worship is an exchange. When we pastor where we are, joining with friends in worship, we are looking for ways to give to each other what God first gives to us.

We are encouraged:

> Let us draw near to God with a sincere heart in full assurance of faith, having our hearts sprinkled to cleanse us from a

168   A Life Worth Becoming

guilty conscience and having our bodies washed with pure water. Let us hold unswervingly to the hope we profess for he who promised is faithful. And let us consider how we may spur one another on towards love and good deeds. Let us not give up meeting together as some are in the habit of doing, but let us encourage one another—and all the more as you see the Day approaching.

In worship, we remind each other of who we are, of the power we possess and of the promise that is ours.

God says that when we participate in life together, beauty surfaces. "You are the light of the world," Jesus said, an image used also of him. "You shine like stars in the universe as you hold out the word of life," Paul adds. It happens because, in the words of Colossians 3:12–14, we clothe ourselves with love. The word picture for clothe is the idea of *getting into*.

I get into Christ. He is in to you.

And Then There Were None

Satan hates what God loves. God births community and the enemy divides it. Friendships bond and the devil breaks them. It is no surprise that relationships of all forms suffer from conflict.

Our intention to love friends and pastor them will be challenged. From a Biblical overview, we can expect those challenges to come from eight different fronts: Deception, jealousy, violence, sexual immorality, pride, grumbling, persecution, and hurtful words. Satan uses each of these to tear at the fabric of our relationships.

For our purposes, we want to focus on three of these threats. As we seek to influence people, our motives will be questioned (deception), our actions will be criticized (grumbling) and our character will be assaulted (hurtful words).

Joseph

First of all, Satan uses deception to disrupt community. The very first human community, God with Adam and Eve, was stained by deception.

Deception always challenges what God said. The serpent asked Eve "Did God really say?" We are reminded to "Let no one deceive you with empty words."

Sometimes the deception comes in the way of teaching. "Watch out for false prophets" Jesus warned. Paul confessed "But I am afraid that just as Eve was deceived by the serpent's cunning, your minds may somehow be led astray from your sincere and pure devotion to Christ. For if someone comes to you and preaches a Jesus other than the Jesus we are preached . . . you put up with it easily enough."

At other times, the deception is masked in our communication with each other. It is why Jesus says "Simply let your 'Yes' be 'Yes', and your 'No', 'No'; anything beyond this comes from the evil one." Paul adds "each of you must put off falsehood and speak truthfully to his neighbor," and "do not lie to each other, since you have taken off your old self with its practices and have put on the new self." The apostles took great pains to convey "For the appeal we make does not spring from error or impure motives, nor are we trying to trick you."

Regardless of the form of the deception, the intent of deception is to lead us astray. Satan doesn't necessarily unravel the whole in one attempt. He pulls at strings. He calls into question God's lead. For example, He doesn't declare "God lied to you." Far more subtly, he questions that we ever heard God right in the first place. Why attack God's credibility when he can more easily undermine our own.

Our best intent will be questioned by our dearest friends, and our character will be brought under a microscope. The belief God had placed in them concerning our heart and motive is under attack. The Apostle Paul, one of the greatest leaders in the early church

170   A Life Worth Becoming

and the primary contributor to the writing of the New Testament, had his motives constantly questioned. This is the context in which Paul writes "for Satan himself masquerades as an angel of light."

In intentional relationship, we will act in a way that will be criticized. Kind David and his men returned to Ziklag and found it destroyed by fire and their families taken captive. "David was greatly distressed because the men were talking of stoning him; each one was bitter in spirit because of his sons and daughters. But David found strength in the Lord his God."

Acts 6:1 reports "In those days when the number of disciples was increasing, the Grecian Jews among them complained against the Hebraic Jews because their widows were being overlooked in the daily distribution of food. So the Twelve gathered all the disciples together and said, "It would not be right for us to neglect the ministry of the word of God in order to wait on tables. Brothers, choose seven men from among you who are full of the Spirit and wisdom. We will turn this responsibility over to them."

Paul warns "Do not grumble, as some of them did—and were killed by the destroying angel."

There are times complaint or distress is well-founded and times it is not. In Acts there was basis for a right complaint, and the apostles initiated a solution. David was as distressed as his men and suffered the same losses, but he was the target of their aggression. He drew near to the one he still had left to turn to. The Israelites grumbled against Moses but they were really mad at God. He wasn't too happy about that. The Greek word for grumbling is the one we derive for the word gong. It speaks of low murmuring or a buzzing among crowds. God despises it.

Sometimes our action or inaction needs correction. Occasionally, we are targets of misplaced frustration. Once in awhile, we take the heat for God.

Joseph 171

In relationship, we get to ask the following. Is my friend's complaint valid and do I need to correct my oversight? Am I simply the target of my friend's frustration and does he need to draw from my faith? Is my friend dealing deeply with God and do I need to pray?

Attack has a progression. Satan wants a person to question motives. Soon the silence of the questions will find voice complaining of someone's action. Then the focus moves from action, which could be corrected, to character that is judged as beyond repair.

Paul pleaded "If you keep on biting and devouring each other, watch out or you will be destroyed by each other." Again, he urged "do not let any unwholesome talk come out of your mouths, but only what is helpful for building others up according to their needs, that it may benefit those who listen."

Peter tells us "Do not repay evil with evil or insult with insult, but with blessing, because to this you were called so that you may inherit a blessing. For whoever would love life and see good days must keep his tongue from evil and his lips from deceitful speech. He must turn from evil and do good; he must seek peace and pursue it."

When friends are so deceived that our character is judged, truth can be our only response. We do not reply in kind. We don't add people on our side. We bless. To bless is to speak the Lord's word for another. We remind people of who they are, and in turn we are also reminding them of what we have done, of who we have been. When our character is judged, our friends have grown short-sighted, and only God's vision of who we are can restore their view.

Even though Satan has been undermining community, love wins. We are intentional in friendship because greater is he who is in us than the evil one who is in the world. We hang out with friends because love covers a multitude of sins. We minister to

172   A Life Worth Becoming

friends and team with them because God is creative and expresses himself through us. We share in experiences with friends because God is resident, and any one moment can become unforgettable.

Above all the distress our friends endure, they see one life-changing conviction in us that carries them through: We see the best in them. We want the best for them.

It was November 20, 1937. Frankie knew he was in trouble. The brakes on the coal car were failing, and it would only be moments before it crashed into the car ahead. Two men, unaware of the runaway car, were cleaning out the remains of the coal from the last load. Death was imminent.

Frankie jumped from the runaway car and raced ahead of it to warn his friends. As impact neared, he jumped back into coal car and gave a last desperate yank on the brake wheel. The brakes were unresponsive, and the car crashed into the other. Frankie was hurled forward and out the left side of the car. He grabbed for a hold with his right arm and the left side of his body slid under the wheels, severing his left leg immediately and crushing his left arm between the wheel and the track.

Frankie would be in and out of the hospital over the next six months. His left leg was missing, and his left arm was gone from below his elbow. He learned to walk with the aid of a crutch. His wife, Margaret, says he never complained about his condition. He was later awarded the Carnegie Medal for the heroism he displayed in saving the lives of his friends.

One day, years later and after Frankie had passed away, his wife was talking to her grandchildren about their grandfather. They were asking questions about how he would get around, how we would garden and work.

"Oh, he just seemed to do it", she answered.

"The hardest thing," she continued, "Was when he carpentered. I'd have to hold the nails for him, and he'd swing the hammer."

Joseph 173

You are picturing this, right? Margaret held nails while her one-armed, one-legged husband swung a framing hammer at both the nail and her fingers.

Frankie was a hero. He saved the lives of two men. Margaret was a hero, too. She held the nail.

We are a people being transformed. We are becoming more like Christ as we follow God's lead prayerfully, Biblically, and freely by faith. We are making a difference in the lives of people as we are intentional in relationship, as we are *there* for them.

The church is being made beautiful because you and I are refusing to disqualify ourselves as effective in ministry, but instead, are giving ourselves to friends in need. This is what heroes are made of. This is trusting love. This is a life worth becoming.

Away From The Lights Of The Stage

Sam Shoemaker helped lay the foundation for Alcoholics Anonymous and was influential in the forming of the Fellowship of Christian Athletes, Young Life, and *Faith at Work* magazine. He was offered many opportunities to work within various religious institutions and systems, and declined each. At times he was criticized for his unwillingness. He answered his critics with the following:

I stay near the door.
I neither go too far in, nor stay too far out,
The door is the most important door in the world—
It is the door through which men walk when they find God.
There's no use my going way inside, and staying there,
When so many are still outside and they, as much as I,
Crave to know where the door is.
And all that so many ever find
Is only the wall where a door ought to be.
They creep along the wall like blind men,
With outstretched, groping hands,
Feeling for a door, knowing there must be a door,
Yet they never find it . . .
So I stay near the door.

The most tremendous thing in the world
Is for me to find that door—the door to God.
The most important thing any man can do

A Life Worth Becoming

Is to take hold of one of those blind, groping hands,
And to put it on the latch—the latch that only clicks
And opens to the man's own touch.
Men die outside that door, as starving beggars die
On cold nights in cruel cities in the dead of winter-
Die for want of what is within their grasp.
They live, on the other side of it—live because they have
    found it.
Nothing else matters compared to helping them find it,
And open it, and walk in, and find Him . . .
So I stay near to door.

Go in, great saints, go all the way in-
Go way down into the cavernous cellars,
And way up into the spacious attics—
It is a vast, roomy house, this house where God is.
Go into the deepest of hidden casements,
Of withdrawal, of silence, of sainthood.
Some must inhabit those inner rooms,
And know the depths and heights of God,
And call outside to the rest of us how wonderful it is.
Sometimes I take a deeper look in,
Sometimes I venture in a little farther;
But my place seems closer to the opening . . .
So I stay near the door.
There is another reason why I stay there.
Some people get part way in and become afraid
Lest God and the zeal of His house devour them;
For God is so very great, and asks all of us.
And these people feel a cosmetic claustrophobia,
And want to get out. "Let me out!" they cry.
And the people way inside only terrify them more.
Somebody must be by the door to tell them that they are spoiled

Joseph 177

For the old life, they have seen too much;
Once taste God, and nothing but God will do any more.
Somebody must be watching for the frightened
Who seek to sneak out just where they came in,
To tell them how much better it is inside.

The people too far in do not see how near these are
To leaving-preoccupied with the wonder of it all.
Somebody must watch for those who have entered the
        door,
But would like to run away. So for them, too,
I stay near the door.
I admire the people who go way in.
But I wish they would not forget how it was
Before they got in. Then they would be able to help
The people who have not yet even found the door,
Or the people who want to run away again from God.
You can go in too deeply, and stay in too long,
And forget the people outside the door.
As for me, I shall take my old accustomed place,
Near enough to God to hear Him, and know He is there,
But not so far from men as not to hear them,
And remember they are there, too.
Where? Outside the door-
Thousands of them, millions of them.
But- more important for me-
One of them, two of them, ten of them,
Whose hands I am intended to put on the latch.
So I shall stay by the door and wait
For those who seek it.
"I had rather be a door keeper in the house of my bed," the
        psalmist said.
So I stay near the door.

A Life Worth Becoming

A pastor friend of mine first shared that poem with me. It rocked my world. It re-captured the heart of what the Lord had given me when I first came to know him: A desire that others know him too.

A Life Worth Becoming is about relational, lifestyle ministry. It is about us making a difference in the lives of people by us becoming more like Jesus, and in the process being more intentional in relationship. This is what defines our ministry. We may still be involved in strategic ministry, those ventures which involve coordination with other people: It is fun to team together. But we prioritize loving those we know directly, people in the course of our every day. God values this.

The opening of Matthew's gospel holds these words: "All this took place to fulfill what the Lord had said through the prophet: The virgin will be with child and will give birth to a son, and they will call him Immanuel—which means, 'God with us.'"

God with us. And by His Spirit, God in us and God through us. When God is in us, his desires become our desires. And he desires lost and lonely people to know and to draw near to him.

One time I was at a conference in Tennessee. It was a beautiful time of year, football season; the color of the leaves divergent and glorious, the air nipped with cool. I had spent the day listening to speakers in outdoor venues. I returned to my hotel later that night and decided to take in the live band that was playing in the bar. As I sat there, I began to engage people in conversation. With each person, I would ask, "Why are you here?" And to the person, each replied "I'm lonely."

I understood loneliness. In high school I had friends, but I was so intense about my faith I was hard to get close to. I didn't mean to keep people at arm's length, but apparently that was a comfortable distance for most. I never forget the night I drove home, pulled into the garage, and broke down in violent tears. I was so lonely.

Joseph 179

Loneliness has many ushers. Some people are lonely through circumstance, some through depression and addiction, and others through strength of personality. No matter the avenue, the venue is the same: A stage of one. Players may come and go, but the curtain falls and the light darkens leaving the single actor alone on stage.

Sin did this. Separation is sin's child, and solitaire is the only game she plays.

Jesus doesn't play solitaire. He sees our need for others and knows it begins with him. He invites us to come out and get some air, explore and exercise, walk, run and ride. It breaks his heart to see one of his kids left alone on the playground.

In Matthew 9:36 it says "When he saw the crowds, he had compassion on them, because they were harassed and helpless, like sheep without a shepherd." The words harassed and helpless are violent words, conveying being skinned and mangled, as well as thrown about and cast down. The words *left for dead* come to mind. As do the words *left alone.*

Jesus' response was not judgment. It was compassion, a word describing the greatest depth of emotion. The word is used elsewhere to describe the father's appeal on behalf of his demon-possessed son, and the father's heart for his prodigal son.

Other people might have responded differently. They may have judged them as deserving of the consequences. After all, "one reaps what one sows" they say to themselves. Or they may have simply passed by, feeling the need too great, their resources too small and their own issues too demanding.

Not Jesus. He saw a people ravaged by sin, play acting at their well-being, fearful of speaking the last line, of hearing the quieting of the crowd's applause, of the darkening of the stage that leaves them alone yet one more time.

Jesus wants to redirect this play. He seeks to rewrite the script. Creative and expressive, Jesus wants to change the entire production.

180   A Life Worth Becoming

In his mind, he sees a whole new set, with fabulous new wardrobe, and a finale to beat all contenders. When his play closes, the actors bow hand in hand together.

We get to assist! We help by doing what Jesus is doing in the lives of our friends. The things we see him do we do also.

What do we see Jesus do? In the gospels, we see Jesus preaching, healing and helping. We are beautiful in the lives of people when we do the same.

The conviction throughout this book is that the beginning point of all effective ministry is relationship, and to pastor friends is a natural lifestyle. Ministry in the Bible is person to person as the need arises. Preaching, which has been professionalized, is also natural communication from one person to another. We have good news to announce. Healing, which has been compartmentalized, is a natural ministry to one in need. We have power to give away. Good deeds, which have been programmed, are the natural initiative of the gracious: We have a love to pass on. Each of these, though naturally expressed, are supernaturally birthed. In the lives of those we love, we are naturally supernatural.

I Have News

When it comes to preaching in the New Testament, everybody is doing it! John the Baptist came preaching in the Desert of Judea. Jesus began to preach "Repent, for the kingdom of heaven is near." Peter preaches, and then in Acts 8 we read "Those who had been scattered preached the word wherever they went. Up until then we could understand this: John the Baptist, Jesus, Peter— these are the big guys. All of a sudden, the church is scattered from Jerusalem because of persecution, and it is the apostles staying behind for awhile and the rest are preaching. Maybe preaching is something everyone can do.

Joseph 181

The word, preach, means *to proclaim.* So far we can handle this—we proclaim a lot of things. We tell people about our favorite restaurants, teams, experiences and entertainment. Preaching is not difficult for us.

The message we preach is determined by context. When I am with my friends discussing football, I can proclaim the greatness of my team. When I am with someone discussing the failure of their relationship, my proclaiming will use different words, tones, and emotion.

Remember, a person's point of need is God's place of courtship. There are some needs I am not equipped to address (generally, they have to do with home repair, technology and mechanics). My preaching is silenced. Hopefully, I can bring in another voice to be heard.

But there are times I have good news to announce: It might be the gospel itself or it might be a piece of God's truth needed at the time. For instance, God's insight on building financial wealth may be as timely to one person as teaching about forgiveness may be to another.

When we pastor where we are, we preach. We proclaim something good to the listener, and what we proclaim is determined by the need of the listener.

Jesus meets a woman at a well and proceeds to tell her everything she ever did. That caught her attention, and Jesus introduced her to the priority of worship in spirit and in truth.

Phillip meets a eunuch who is reading Scripture and doesn't understand its meaning. Beginning with that passage, Phillip introduces the man to Jesus and baptizes him.

God wants us to speak up for him.

One day I was driving past a Barnes and Noble bookstore. I noticed a church van from a nearby city in the parking lot. In my spirit I heard "Go into the store. In the self-help section you will

182   A Life Worth Becoming

find that pastor reading a book on sexuality." So I went into the store. I walked past the appropriate aisle and saw a man taking sneaky looks in a book (illustrated). Afterwards, I went to the office and phoned the church. I described the man to the receptionist and she confirmed that he worked there on staff. I said nothing other than to ask her to have him phone me. He did. I explained what I had been led to do and said, "God loves you. If you are struggling about something and need to talk I am available to help. I don't think the Lord would have done this unless he wanted you to know how much he loves you and is watching out for you." This pastor took the opportunity to share some things with me and we talked and prayed.

The Bible gives us four guidelines in talking for God.

Speak. Paul said "Unlike so many, we do not peddle the word of God for profit. On the contrary, in Christ we speak before God with sincerity, like men sent from God." The word speak implies a natural conversation. It is simply to say something.

Answer. Peter teaches us to "always be prepared to give an answer to everyone who asks you to give the reason for the hope that you have." The word answer is used elsewhere to mean defense. In other words, we have good reason for what we believe. Defense is different than defensive. That is why Peter continues to say that our answer is to be with gentleness and respect. When asked, we give the reason why Christ is Lord of our life. If love has laid the foundation, truth and honesty will build the relationship.

Proclaim. "We proclaim him, admonishing every man and teaching every man with all wisdom so that we may present everyone perfect in Christ." To admonish is to correct or warn with instruction. When I phoned the pastor from the bookstore, I was admonishing him. It wasn't a judgment without opportunity for response, but a caution with an invitation for discussion. Teaching refers to positive instruction, and so the two are inseparable—we

Joseph 183

do not admonish without positive instruction. Together, the two allow us to become whole or complete (the meaning of the word "perfect").

Persuade. Paul wrote "we try to persuade men." To persuade is to convince and win over. The word war/warfare in the New Testament is written about the context of the mind. The mind is the battleground of spiritual warfare. When Paul says we are not unaware of Satan's schemes, the root of the word schemes means *mind* and refers to confusion and deception. We persuade people when the need of the moment calls for confronting lies they have believed and explaining truths that will set them free.

You too can preach! You have good news for people, news that can be simply shared, clearly answered, positively imparted and convincingly given. Whether shared in whole or in part, dealing with life issues or deep questions about faith, God so believes in you he speaks up through you.

The life worth becoming engages friends in conversation. We don't set them up for a presentation. We join them and apply truth to their situation, not as an outside expert but as an up-close friend who has experienced something of the same. There is no more powerful dynamic, or greater testimony, than someone being able to say of us "I can talk to them about anything."

Naturally Supernatural

Healing intimidates us. We don't like the questions that surround it, such as "Why does God heal some and not all?" Some of the characters and showmanship associated with public healing scare us. One of the most beautiful moments in human history—God intervening with power to meet need—has been tainted and scarred through greed, insincerity and manipulation. It is a definite part of the script God will rewrite.

184   A Life Worth Becoming

But we cannot allow our concern about healing outweigh our concern about another's need. Compassion must triumph over question.

When the Pharisees criticized Jesus for healing on the Sabbath, he responded "You hypocrites! Doesn't each of you on the Sabbath untie his ox or donkey from the stall and lead it out to give it water? Then should not this woman, a daughter of Abraham, whom Satan has kept bound for eighteen long years, be set free on the Sabbath day from what bound her."

Jesus is very serious about healing.

And people are very responsive to healing. People in need of help came to Jesus for healing. "News about him spread all over Syria, and people brought to him all who were ill with various diseases . . . and he healed them." And, "the people were delighted with all the wonderful things he was doing."

Several years ago I directed a summer camp for high school students. The churches represented didn't consider themselves to be charismatic. At the camp, God had the audacity to physically heal some of the kids that people prayed for. Afterwards, at an evaluation session of the camp directors, an agenda item was listed as "the healing problem". Apparently some of the church leaders weren't very happy with us. Funny, but the kids that were healed didn't complain.

I've never had one of my unbelieving friends become offended when I told them I would pray for them. I imagine you might know some that would be, and of course you would be sensitive to them. But I've let businessmen, neighbors, students, prostitutes and crooks know that I was praying for them, all people I care about, and I also tell them what I was led to pray for. It's been an awesome day when those prayers were answered.

They don't mind because they know me.

Joseph   185

When we speak of healing, we aren't referring to physical illness alone. Healing occurs anytime the Lord intervenes and restores. Illnesses are healed. Demons are defeated. Certain calamity is avoided. Miracle describes God's intervention; healing describes the result.

We can be naturally supernatural.

We love our friends, and they love us. Regardless of whether they follow Jesus or not, his heart is romancing theirs through ours. They taste what it is to love God by loving us. Being ourselves in relationship with our friends is critical, and if Christ is in you, you are supernatural. What that looks like differs with each person.

I was once hired to work in a company. When the existing staff found out I had been a pastor, they groaned and one person was quoted as saying "I feel judged already." The first day I reported, I was carrying a notebook that someone thought was a Bible. The rumors started flying. I responded by staying true to myself, accepting people as they were, hanging out with them and joking around with them. When I left, I missed them and they missed me. A kinship had developed, and within it I had opportunity to lead a person to Christ and to encourage the believers that were there.

Sometimes we speak up for God without announcing it is his words being spoken. At times we pray without any drum roll or recognition. Many times we serve and people see our kindness without knowing God's initiative. Jesus will get the glory, but he doesn't always require the initial credit.

On the other hand, certain times are groomed for clarity. We say things like "Let me show you what God says about forgiveness." We promise "I will pray for you", and better, "let me pray with you." We tell our neighbor "I love you but God loves you more", and then show up with friends to do some good.

God intervenes with miracles; healing results.

For Goodness Sake

> God gave himself for us to redeem us from all wickedness and to purify for himself a people that are his very own, eager to do what is good.

One time I was prayerfully thinking through the wedding at Cana. Jesus and his disciples attended, and at one point the wedding party ran out of wine. This was a great embarrassment to the wedding party, a cultural faux pas the family would not live down. They were much more serious about their wedding parties than we are.

Jesus took care of it. He turned water into wine, and his tasted better than theirs.

While praying, I asked God "Why?" I know the text says this is the first of his miraculous signs, and that the disciples put their faith in him. But he didn't attend the wedding intending to do this. He even told his mom his time had not yet come. That it was his first sign was the result but not the reason for the miracle. So, again, I asked God "Why?"

"Because I'm nice," is what I heard. I will never forget the moment or the words. Question my sanity if you like, but you can't question my theology. Besides, I've been a lot nicer since than.

"Nice" is effective ministry. In the teaching of the sheep and the goats, Jesus makes clear that nice is necessary:

> Lord, when did we see you hungry and feed you, or thirsty and give you something to drink? When did we see you a stranger and invite you in, or needing clothes and clothe you? When did we see you sick or in prison and go to visit you?" The King will reply, "Whatever you did for the least of these brothers of mine, you did for me." Later, to those who did not help, he says "whatever you did not do for one of the least of these, you did not do for me."

Joseph 187

I didn't like those verses for the longest time. My public ministry gifts were proof enough that I was a giver. Measuring my self against feeding the hungry and clothing the poor would only have revealed a self-centeredness I had kept well-hidden. No, I avoided that text.

But God would have none of that. Through a series of events God taught me that nice is as meaningful to him as gifted. When I resigned from the last local church I served, I knew that my public preaching was about to enter a silent time. However, I also knew that my private, personal ministry was about to be stepped up. And I had come to understand that either ministry was of equal worship in God's eyes. That's really all that matters, isn't it?

Look at what happens when we are nice:

- Live such good lives among the pagans that, tough they accuse you of doing wrong, they may see your good deeds and glorify God on the day he visits us. I Peter 2:12
- And do not forget to do good and to share with others, for with such sacrifices God is pleased. Hebrews 13:16

Beauty has been a theme throughout this book. We are beautiful in the lives of others as we give away what God gives through us. Sometimes, our beauty is crowned when we are called to give the ultimate gift.

On May 9, 2006, Petty Officer 2nd Class Michael A. Monsoor, risked his life when he and a fellow Navy SEAL pulled another team member shot in the leg to safety while bullets shot past them. Both soldiers would be awarded the Silver Star for their actions.

75% of Navy SEAL candidates drop out of training, notorious for "Hell Week", a five-day stint of continual drills broken by only four hours sleep total. Michael passed training on his second attempt.

188   A Life Worth Becoming

As a SEAL, he was extremely disciplined and accomplished, yet Michael had always been considered by his team to be a humble man who drew strength from his family and faith.

On September 29, 2006, Iraqi insurgents tossed a grenade into a sniper hideout, striking Michael's chest and bouncing to the floor.

"He never took his eye off the grenade, his only movement was down toward it," said a 28-year-old lieutenant. "He undoubtedly saved mine and the other SEAL's lives, and we owe him."

This time, Michael Monsoor was killed.

What impresses me about Michael's story is that he didn't hesitate. A different training drove him as well, and his sacrifice was made in the shadow of the cross. He was a tough guy. And he loved his friends well. Beauty couldn't be more attractive than that.

Where True Beauty
Is Displayed

John Ortberg ranks high on my list of favorite teachers. In his book *Love Beyond Reason,* he writes:

One of the strangest houses in the United States is known as the Winchester House, in the Bay area. It was built by Mrs. Winchester, whose husband's wealth came from the rifle associated with their name. Mrs. Winchester lost her husband and her only child, and out of grief or guilt or reasons now lost to time she became obsessed with the occult. She embarked on a massive building project apparently based on the belief that as long as she continued to build her house she would never die.

It is an extraordinary structure. Its construction occupied sixteen carpenters employed full-time for thirty-eight years. At its largest (it has since been partly destroyed by fire), it contained 2,000 doors and 160,000 windows—more than the Empire State Building. The front doors were installed at the then-staggering sum of $3,000. They were used only one time—by the men who installed them. There were twists and turns at every hand; secret passageways and hidden corridors and other eccentricities that are harder to fathom: stairs that run to the ceiling and no further, doors that open only into brick walls. All this was done apparently to confuse Death.

She was still building when Death came, and Death was not confused at all. Death has a wonderful sense of direction.

After Mrs. Winchester died it took eight trucks working full-time every day six and a half weeks to haul away the building materials and excess junk out of that house. For thirty-eight years

189

they had been coming, and then they came once more. They came for her.

"For God so loved the world, he gave his only Son that whoever would believe on him would not perish but would have eternal life". This verse presents the end of your story and the beginning of your life. He has saved you, not only into eternity but into relationship with him. And you love him.

Some of your friends believe as you do, and others not yet. Regardless, each of them has been entrusted to you. You are to pastor them.

Through you, people see God and experience his grace. You are in the process of becoming like Jesus, and in your genuine relationship with others they come to understand that what is true for you might be real for them too.

As a result of this reading, you have affirmed that God is expressing himself in you through grace, friendship and innovation. He is cultivating each by leading you into personal transformation, intentional relationship and lifestyle ministry.

From Initiative to Influence

By faith we understand that the universe was formed at God's command, so that what is seen was not made out of what was visible.

God is in the business of making something out of nothing. He is creative. The Bible says we are his workmanship. He is placing himself on display by what he creates in us. He initiates our growth and authors our ministry.

Abraham is a great example of God's creativity. The bible says Abraham "is our father in the sight of God, in whom he believed—

Joseph 191

the God who gives life to the dead and calls things that are not as though they were".

Do you know his story? He was first named Abram, and God changed his name to Abraham, which means "father of many". Small problem: At the time God changed his name he was impotent. In Hebrew, names had meaning. So when Abraham would introduce himself to a fellow Hebrew, that person heard Abraham say "Hello, I am Father of Many." To which, of course, a person would ask, "Wow, how many children do you have?"

"Uh, none," Abraham would reply. This was an issue. (Actually, he had one, but it was with a woman not his wife. Things were a little tense).

Abraham *had an identity and nothing to show for it.*

Do you ever feel this way? You are his workmanship. You are called to pastor where you are. You are the key to the transformation of his church and the increasing effectiveness of her ministry. You have a promise from God. And today, you may have very little to show for it. Yet, God is creative.

Do not disbelieve God. He believes in you. You have more than potential. You have promise.

Abraham had a second issue. *He had a promise, and no power of his own to fulfill it.* The Bible says "Against all hope, Abraham in hope believed and so became the father of many nations. . . . Without weakening in his faith, he faced the fact that his body was as good as dead—since he was about a hundred years old—and that Sarah's womb was also dead. Yet he did not waver through unbelief regarding the promise of God, but was strengthened in his faith and gave glory to God, being fully persuaded that God had power to do what he had promised."

Sometimes we forget that when we belong to Jesus we have the Spirit of God resident in us. We try to do good things for God in our own strength. However, the one thing true about a promise from God is that we have no power to make it happen. He has to keep it by his strength, not ours.

You have a promise, and you have no power to fulfill it. You long to make a difference in people's lives. You have a vision that a team of people would love to join you in. You desire to serve, but you don't want to fall short of expectations. You seek to lead, but fear you will come up empty in ability. God can keep his promise.

Think with me about Abraham again. I don't want to be inappropriate in our reflection, but how did Abraham know the time had come for God to keep his promise? Apparently, one night he and Sarah were home, reclining in their rockers, he impotent and she barren. He looked at his wife. Passion began to surface. It was time. He told her to put in her teeth and take off her clothes. He became potent. She became pregnant.

How will you know it is time? Opportunity will come, and you won't be able to ignore a stirring in your spirit to act. You will be led to pray for someone. You will pick up the phone and call someone out of the blue. You will say yes to a volunteer effort. You will be inclined to write a person. You will give sacrificially.

God intended for true beauty to be displayed apart from the stage. When I speak, I dance with God. There is rarely a time like it for me, and I enjoy every opportunity. But the platform is not the primary place God displays his beauty through me. That place would be in relationship, in the lives of people to whom I am giving and forgiving. I pray that I might always have opportunity for public gifts. I pray more that I am unforgettable in the hearts of people I love.

When I coach people in relational, lifestyle ministry, I ask them to pray and make a list of people they believe God has entrusted to them to pastor. It's usually not a long list at all. After they

Joseph 193

have identified them, I encourage them to calendar times they will pray for their friends. It doesn't matter if it's once a day, once a week or once a month. It's what the Lord leads that matters, and that they are intentional to do what he leads.

After they have prayed for them, I encourage them to follow up how they prayed for a person with conversation. One doesn't have to say "I prayed for you." (Even though I probably would). It may be more appropriate to just start talking about what came up in prayer. For example, let's say you prayed for a co-worker, and sensed they were nervous about an upcoming interview for a promotion. If they don't yet know the Lord, it's effective to approach them and ask, "Hey, how are you feeling about the interview?" Obviously, if they do know the Lord, it's encouraging to tell them you were praying for them and sensed their anxiety. Believers will see your prayer as mail from God. Unbelievers will see your conversation as love. Both work just fine.

I then encourage people to calendar times of encouragement. It's sometimes easy for people to coincide their prayer with an expression of encouragement, but some people keep them as separate calendar events. Encouragement takes many forms, but in essence it communicates thoughtfulness and generosity. A word well spoken, a gift well timed, an event shared—all are the heart of the Spirit visibly expressed by you.

Finally, I help people to see there are times they are called to resource people they pastor. Is there a way you can help a friend reach a goal? Is there something you can do for your friend they cannot do for their self? Is there someone or something else you can introduce to your friend that will help them in a time of need?

To pastor where you are means to pray for, encourage and resource people you love.

194   A Life Worth Becoming

Passing The Baton

When I speak with leaders of the church, I encourage them to reorient their strategies so that the starting point of ministry is people and their relationships.

There will always be a place for shared ministry in the church: Efforts that require a team of people and coordination of activity. Today, though, ministry coaching needs to orient itself around personal transformation, intentional relationship and lifestyle ministry.

Leaders have new questions before them:

1. How will we encourage spiritual growth as a process?
2. Can we present spiritual disciplines in a way that facilitate rather than define spiritual maturity?
3. How will we give room for repentance? Will it be possible for leaders in our church to talk about their own process without being set up for criticism in return?
4. How will we help people recognize their natural network of relationships?
5. Can small group ministries transition from its current structures to a more fluid strategy of coaching people to be intentional in community with those with whom they already have relationship?
6. Will we celebrate those who influence people but don't serve in program elements of the church? What will be our stories?
7. What does a more fluid, relational ministry mean for the budget?
8. What changes in staffing will result from a greater emphasis on coaching?
9. Will we be more concerned with the size of the congregation when gathered or the influence of the congregation when apart?

Joseph

The church to come is more fluid, agile and influential because it is more responsive, personal and relational.

The church ahead will be led by teams of coaches whose effectiveness is defined by the accomplishments of those they serve.

The church my kids and grandkids lead will be an influence in the community not an institution on the corner.

In the end, our final word is simple. God's church is beautiful. It begins with the individual who is becoming more like Jesus through being in love with him. Such love expresses itself in relationship with others. By partnering with God in the lives of others, we give a grace they would not know otherwise. God is real to them.

We are not alone, and the church gathered is a place of support. We practice on each other. We learn together. We become one voice in worship to the Lover.

The value of this simplicity can never be reduced. Leaders who understand it will change everything they must to facilitate it. The church is not a show. It is not a system. It is more than any one strategy. It is about people—in their homes, neighborhoods and workplace—seeking God to display himself through them.

Jesus said, "The kingdom of heaven is like yeast that a woman took and mixed into a large amount of flour *until it worked all through the dough* (italics mine)."

He is working you, and He is working us, into the lives of people, throughout our societies, into the very essence of our cultures.

Through our simple acts of love, people will never be the same.

Information please

In the book *A 3ʳᵈ Serving of Chicken Soup for the Soul,* Paul Villiard has a story included that I've never forgotten.

He tells of the time his family had one of the first telephones in the neighborhood. Its polished oak case hung on the wall.

196   A Life Worth Becoming

He was fascinated to discover that somewhere in that phone lived a wonderful person named "Information Please". She knew everything, and could even tell you the right time or give you another person's number.

> One day Paul was playing in the basement when he hit his finger with a hammer. No one was home, so he ran to the telephone.
> Climbing up, I unhooked the receiver and held it to my ear. "Information Please," I said into the mouthpiece just above my head.
> A click or two, and a small clear voice spoke into my ear. "Information."
> "I hurt my finger" I wailed into the phone . . . I hit it with the hammer and it hurts."
> "Then chip off a little piece of ice and hold it on your finger. That will stop the hurt."
> After that, I called Information Please for everything.
> And there was the time that Petey, our pet canary, died. I called Information Please and told her the sad story . . . She must have sensed my deep concern, for she said quietly, "Paul, always remember that there are other worlds to sing in."

Paul explains that all this took place in a small town in the Pacific Northwest. When he was nine years old he moved to Boston and missed his mentor.

Years later, on his way to college, his plane touched down in Seattle. Without really thinking, he dialed his hometown operator and said, "Information Please." Miraculously, he heard the familiar voice: "Information."

Paul expressed to her how much he missed her, and she explained that she always looked forward to his calls. She didn't have children of her own. They promised to stay in touch, and she told him when he called to just ask for Sally.

Joseph   197

Three months later, Paul was back in Seattle and dialed the operator. A different voice answered "Information." Paul asked for Sally.

"Are you a friend?"

"Yes," I said, "An old friend."

"Then I'm sorry to have to tell you. . . . Sally had only been working part-time the last few years because she was ill. She died five weeks ago." Before I could hang up, she said, "Wait a minute. Did you say your name was Villiard?"

"Yes."

"Well, Sally left a message for you. She wrote it down."

"Tell him I still say there are other worlds to sing in. He'll know what I mean."

There is another world to sing in. The life worth becoming leads the chorus, gives voice to its tune, and becomes the song people can't get out of their head.

Endnotes

Introduction

1. Source: Maggie Troyer, used by permission. Thank you Maggie and Rich.
2. "workmanship": Ephesians 2:10
3. "intent": Ephesians 3:10
4. "attractive" Titus 2:10
5. Mark 2:1–12
6. Mark 2:13–15
7. Michael Yaconelli, *Dangerous Wonder* (Colorado Springs: Navpress, 1998), 47
8. Mark 2:15–17
9. Mark 2:27
10. Thank you John Honold

Chapter One: I Want You

11. Gladiator, Dreamworks
12. As told to me by Steve Ridgeway
13. Everybody Loves Raymond sitcom, Season 3
14. In Immanuel's Land by Anne Rose Cousin from the writings of Samuel Rutherford, www.jithy.com/immanuels_land.htm
15. "full of grace and truth": John 1:14–18

200   A Life Worth Becoming

16. "rich in mercy": Ephesians 2:4–5
17. "man and his wife heard": Genesis 3:9
18. "Spirit and the bride": Revelation 22:17
19. "all have sinned": Romans 3:23
20. From *Ringing ballads, including Curfew must not ring tonight,* Rose Hartwick Thorpe, 1887 womenshistory.about.com/library/etext/poem1/blp_thorpe_curfew.htm
21. "do not set aside": Galatians 2:21
22. "After beginning": Galatians 3:3
23. Eugene Peterson, *Leap Over A Wall* (San Francisco: HarperCollins, 1997), 206
24. "made coverings": Genesis 3:7,8
25. Harry Schaumber, *False Intimacy* (Colorado Springs: Navpress, 1997)
26. Michael Yaconelli, *Dangerous Wonder* (Colorado Sprins: Navpress, 1998), 121
27. Max Lucado, *A Love Worth Giving* (Nashville: W Publishing Group, 2002), 46
28. "If God is for us": Romans 8:31–35
29. Mark 2:13
30. "I pray that":Ephesians 3:16
31. "incomparably great power": Ephesians 1:19
32. "God opposes": James 4:6
33. Jack Canfield, Mark Victor Hansen, *A 2nd Helping of Chicken Soup for the Soul* (Deerfield Beach, Fl.: Health Communications Inc., 1995), 24–27
34. "Stephen": Acts 6:8
35. "Paul and Barnabas": Acts 14:3
36. "He who did not": Romans 8:32
37. "The Lord is my shepherd": Psalm 23:1
38. "all these things": Matthew 6:33

Joseph   201

39. "my God will meet" Philippians 4:19
40. "If you then": Matthew 7:11
41. "Be kind": Ephesians 4:32
42. "He forgave us": Colossians 2:13–15
43. Handout from Lee Strobel, Willow Creek Community Church conference, May 1997
44. "Entirely on their own": 2 Corinthians 8:3–9
45. "Now to each one": I Corinthians 12:6,7
46. "With great power": Acts 4:22
47. "I will not venture": Romans 15:18,19
48. "All these": I Corinthians 12:11
49. "act of grace": 2 Corinthians 8:6,7
50. Philip Yancey, *What's So Amazing About Grace?* (Grand Rapids: Zondervan, 1997), 48–49
51. "Let your conversation": Colossians 4:6
52. Jack Canfield et al, *A Second Chicken Soup for the Woman's Soul* (Deerfield Beach, Fl.: Health Communications Inc., 1998), 12–15

Chapter 2: But Not To Myself Alone

53. "I know longer call you": John 15:15
54. "A friend": Proverbs 17:17
55. "sticks closer": Proverbs 18:24
56. "pleasantness": Proverbs 27:9
57. "pure heart": Proverbs 22:11
58. "covers over an offense": Proverbs 17:9
59. Ron Mehl, *The Tender Commandments* (Portland: Multnomah, 2001)
60. "Two are better than one": Ecclesiastes 4:9–12
61. "Better is open": Proverbs 27:5–6

202   A Life Worth Becoming

62. "spreading a tent":Proverbs 29:5
63. "As iron": Proverbs 27:17
64. "Brothers": Galatians 6:1
65. "If your brother": Matthew 18:15
66. Galatians 2:11–14
67. "Carry": Galatians 6:2
68. source unknown
69. "A man of many": Proverbs 18:24

Chapter 3: That New Might Come

70. Alice Gray, *Stories for a Man's Heart* (Sisters, OR: Multnomah, 1999), 25–26
71. *Be All You Can Be*
72. Mark 2:18–20
73. Mark 2:19
74. Mark 2:21–22
75. source unknown
76. Dietrich Bonhoeffer, *Ethics* (Touchstone, 1995)
77. Mark 2:17
78. Mark 2:23–28
79. source unknown

Chapter 4: First Within Me

80. Michael Yaconelli, *Dangerous Wonder* (Colorado Springs: Navpress, 1998), 118–119
81. Matthew 5:3–12
82. "This poor man": Psalm 34:6
83. Luke 18:2,3
84. Luke 18:9–14

Joseph   **203**

85. "These people": Matthew 15:8
86. "like newborn babies": I Peter 2:1–2
87. "take a stand": Ephesians 6:11
88. source unknown
89. Steve Farrar, *Finishing Strong* (Portland: Multnomah, 2000)
90. "the Son can do nothing by himself": John 5:19
91. "anyone who has faith": John 14:12
92. On Joseph, see Matthew 2
93. "During the days": Hebrews 5:7
94. Alice Gray, *Stories for the Heart* (Gresham, OR: Vision House, 1996), 62–63
95. "strong in spirit": Luke 1:80
96. "inner being": Ephesians 3:16
97. "We have this treasure": 2 Corinthians 4:7–9
98. As told to me by Dennis Easter
99. "Be on your guard": I Corinthians 16:13–14
100. "be strong": Ephesians 6:10,12
101. "I will build": Matthew 16:18

Chapter 5: Then Through Me

102. "I will ask": John 14:16, 26
103. "all baptized": I Corinthians 12:13
104. "be filled": Ephesians 5:18
105. "keep in step": Galatians 5:25
106. "all filled": Acts 4:31
107. "on all occasions": Ephesians 6:18
108. "worship by the Spirit": Philippians 3:3
109. "keep in step": Galatians 5:25
110. Tony Campolo, citation unknown

204　　　A Life Worth Becoming

111. "by his power": 2 Thessalonians 1:11
112. *Building A Solid Team,* 182–183

Chapter 6: My Heart As Yours

113. Meet The Parents, Dreamworks
114. "house of prayer": Matthew 21:13
115. "spirit and truth": John 4:23,24
116. "led by the Spirit": Romans 8:14
117. Alice Gray, *Stories for a Woman's Heart* (Sisters, OR: Multnomah, 1999), 131
118. "My Father": John 5:17
119. "pray in the Spirit": Ephesians 6:18
120. Jack Canfield, Mark Victor Hansen, *A 6th Bowl of Chicken Soup for the Soul* (Deerbeach, Fl: Health Communications Inc., 1999), 343
121. "In my distress": Psalm 18:6
122. "with loud cries": Hebrews 5:7
123. "Do not be anxious": Philippians 4:6
124. Leonard Ravenhill, *Why Revival Tarries* (Minneapolis: Bethany House, 1979)
125. "Now, Lord": Acts 4:23
126. As told to me by Bob Logan
127. "first of all": I Timothy 2:1–4
128. On Peter in prison, see Acts 12

Chapter 7: Your Words As Mine

129. "devoted": Acts 2:42
130. "devote yourself to": I Timothy 4:13
131. "book of the law": Deuteronomy 31:24

Joseph 205

132. "law on the scroll": Deuteronomy 17:18
133. "All Scripture": 2 Timothy 3:16
134. "These are the commands": Deuteronomy 6:1
135. "If he called": John 10:35
136. "Above all": I Peter 1:20,21
137. "Bear in mind": 2 Peter 3:15,16
138. "You diligently study": John 6:39–40
139. "more noble character": Acts 17:11
140. "stand firm": 2 Thessalonians 2:15
141. Eugene Peterson, *Leap Over a Wall* (San Francisco: Harper Collins, 1997), 190
142. "I myself": Romans 15:14
143. "Let the word": Colossians 3:16
144. "Command certain men": I Timothy 1:3–4
145. "Warn them": 2 Timothy 2:14,16
146. Tony Campolo, *Let Me Tell You A Story* (W Publishing Group, 2000), 65,66

Chapter 8: Unleashed. Unstoppable.

147. Rodney L. Cooper, Ph.D. *Double Bind* (Grand Rapids: Zondervan)
148. Song lyric from Hotel California, The Eagles
149. "The only thing": Galatians 5:6
150. "Through him": Romans 1:5
151. "They tell how": I Thessalonians 1:9
152. "I long to see you": Romans 1:11
153. Thank you Wallace Wartick
154. "After beginning": Galatians 3:3
155. "Without faith": Hebrews 11:6
156. "when warned": Hebrews 11:7

A Life Worth Becoming

157. Quoted in Leadership Journal, edition unknown
158. "obeyed and went": Hebrews 11:8–10
159. Jack Canfield, *The Aladdin Factor* (New York: Berkley Trade, 1995) 97
160. "Abraham reasoned": Hebrews 11:19
161. "God is able": 2 Corinthians 8:8,11
162. "By faith Jacob": Hebrews 11:21–22
163. "saw he was no ordinary": Hebrews 11:23–28
164. Ron Mehl, *The Cure For A Troubled Heart* (Portland: Multnomah, 1996)
165. "passed through the Red Sea": Hebrews 11:29
166. "Obey your leaders": Hebrews 11:17
167. "It is for freedom": Galatians 5:1
168. "everyone who sins": John 8:34–36
169. "Now the Lord": 2 Corinthians 3:17
170. "For sin": Romans 6:14,17,18
171. "To those under": I Corinthians 9:20–21
172. "Christ is the end of the law": Romans 10:4
173. "grace and truth": John 1:17
174. Steve Farrar, *Finishing Strong* (Portland: Multnomah, 2000), 209–210
175. source unknown
176. Reader's Digest, "My Daddy Will Save Me", Peter Michelmore, issue unknown

Chapter 9: I Will Trust Love

177. Larry Crabb, *Connecting* (Nashville: Word, 1997), xiii
178. "Love is patient": I Corinthians 13:4
179. "He is patient": 2 Peter 3:9,15
180. On Lot, see Genesis 13

Joseph 207

181. "They have credited": I Samuel 18:8–9
182. "Love always protects": I Corinthians 13:7
183. "God is with you": Genesis 21:22
184. "But Jesus would not entrust": John 2:24,25
185. "But Barnabas": Acts 9:27–28
186. "Each man should give": 2 Corinthians 9:7
187. "The people rejoiced": I Chronicles 29:9
188. "Go back to your mistress": Genesis 16:9
189. "When Silas": Acts 18:5
190. "A generous man": Proverbs 11:25
191. For Jesus at the wedding, see John 2
192. "We have different gifts": Romans 12:6–8
193. Charles Swindoll, *The Grace Awakening* (Thomas Nelson, 2003)
194. "as each part": Ephesians 4:16
195. "What you are doing": Exodus 18:17–22
196. "The harvest": Matthew 9:37
197. "gave authority": Matthew 10:1–2
198. "appointed": Luke 10:1–2
199. Roy Croft, *The Best Loved Poems of the American People*
200. "Go, therefore": Matthew 28:18–20
201. "What you heard": I Timothy 1:13, 14; 2:2
202. "I no longer call": John 15:15–17
203. "After that whole generation": Judges 2:10–11
204. "King Hezekiah": 2 Chronicles 32:20–23
205. "Let us draw near": Hebrews 10:22–25
206. "light of the world": Matthew 5:14
207. "shine like stars": Philippians 2:15
208. "clothe": Colossians 3:12–14
209. "Did God": Genesis 3:1
210. "Let no one": Ephesians 5:6
211. "Watch out": Matthew 7:15

208   A Life Worth Becoming

212. "But I am afraid": 2 Corinthians 11:3,4
213. "yes": Matthew 6:37
214. "put off falsehood": Ephesians 4:25
215. "do not lie": Colossians 3:9
216. "For the appeal": I Thessalonians 2:3
217. "David was": I Samuel 30:6
218. "In those days": Acts 6:1
219. "Do not grumble": I Corinthians 10:10
220. "If you keep": Galatians 5:15
221. "unwholesome talk": Ephesians 4:29
222. "Do not repay": I Peter 3:9

Chapter 10: Away From The Lights Of The Stage

223. Given to me by Joe Wittwer of Spokane, WA. Thank you, Joe
224. "Immanuel": Matthew 1:22,23
225. "When he saw": Matthew 9:36
226. "scattered": Acts 8:4
227. The woman at the well, John 4
228. Phillip, Acts 8
229. "Unlike so many": 2 Corinthians 2:17
230. "always be prepared": I Peter 3:15
231. "admonish": Colossians 1:28
232. "persuade": 2 Corinthians 5:11
233. "You hypocrites": Luke 13:15,16
234. "News": Matthew 4:24
235. "people were delighted": Luke 13:17
236. "chosen people": I Peter 2:9
237. "gave himself": Titus 2:14

238. Matthew 25:31–46
239. "Live such good lives": I Peter 2:12
240. "do not forget": Hebrews 13:16
241. MSNBC.com/ The Associated Press, October 14, 2006

Conclusion: Where True Beauty Is Displayed

242. John Ortberg, *Love Beyond Reason* (Grand Rapids: Zondervan, 1998), 89–90
243. "God so loved": John 3:16
244. "By faith we understand": Hebrews 11:3
245. "The kingdom of heaven": Matthew 13:33
246. Jack Canfield, Mark Victor Hansen, *A 3rd Serving of Chicken Soup for the Soul* (Deerfield Beach: Fl., 1996), 14–18